An Excellent Life

An Excellent Life

One Family's Experience with Traumatic Injury

Jody Cramer

With a foreword by James Brady

Bloomington, IN Milton Keynes, UK

AuthorHouse™
1663 Liberty Drive, Suite 200
Bloomington, IN 47403
www.authorhouse.com
Phone: 1-800-839-8640

AuthorHouse™ UK Ltd.
500 Avebury Boulevard
Central Milton Keynes, MK9 2BE
www.authorhouse.co.uk
Phone: 08001974150

First published by AuthorHouse 1/24/2006

ISBN: 1-4208-6608-7 (e)
ISBN: 1-4208-5189-6 (sc)

Library of Congress Control Number: 2005903657

Printed in the United States of America
Bloomington, Indiana

This book is printed on acid-free paper.

for Joseph Kirk Lambinas

Contents

Foreword

by James Brady
Chairman, Brain Injury Association and
Former White House Press Secretary
to President Ronald Reagan

An estimated 5.3 million Americans currently live with disability caused by traumatic brain injury (TBI). Each year in the United States alone, 80,000 people experience the onset of long-term disability following a TBI. Vehicle crashes—accounting for 50 percent of all TBIs—are the leading cause of brain injury.

On August 20, 1994, Michael Bethune joined that population. Almost instantaneously, Michael's life and the lives of those closest to him changed forever. In a split second, hospitals, IV tubes, CT scans, therapists, rehabilitation and insurance companies became a regular part of day-to-day life for Michael, his family and friends. On that day, they learned firsthand what it means to be impacted by the "silent epidemic" of brain injury.

With those changes come new experiences, many of them challenging. Life for a person with TBI is not easy. He or she will probably not live what some may call a "normal" life. Rehabilitation—and the cost of that rehabilitation—is extensive. Many hours are spent working with what I playfully term as "physical terrorists"—those persons who work one-on-one with the person with the TBI to regain physical and mental function. Shouts are uttered, screams are blurted out, and many tears are shed as that person tries to regain control of his or her life.

Family dynamics change as well. Sometimes relationships get strained and things fall apart. But more often than not, a family member sustaining a brain injury provides an immediate opportunity for friends and family to grow closer together. All of a sudden, families must work as a team to help provide the love, care and support that is sorely needed. After sustaining my brain injury in 1982, my wife Sarah and I grew closer. Just like Jody Cramer and her family, Sarah had to learn about brain injury and brain injury rehabilitation. She had to learn how to help care for me. She had to learn to demand what was best for me from doctors, therapists and other professionals who specialize in brain injury treatment.

Perhaps one of the most difficult parts about sustaining a brain injury is people telling you just to "get on with life." Brain injury is a major public health concern understood by few. Many times the injuries are internal, giving the appearance that nothing is wrong. Insurance companies, doctors, nurses and other who don't understand and/or specialize in brain injury are often unwilling to provide the necessary care. Unfortunately, persons with brain injury and their families are frequently left to their own devices, feeling like they are the only ones who believe they need more services and support than they are currently receiving.

People often wonder how I was able to make it through and adapt to my "new" life, which is life post-TBI. The fact of the matter is that it requires sheer will and resolve. Looking at the cup and seeing it as half empty will never suffice in recovery from brain injury. Positive attitudes are a must.

Surrounding yourself with positive, playful, loving, caring, hard-working and dedicated people while implementing those attributes into your own life is the only way to come out a winner in situation like this.

Michael, Jody and the rest of their close family and friends certainly have taken that approach. Their story is one of triumphant joys and successes following much hard work and dedication. People reading this book will come to realize that Michael and Jody's strategies of coping with brain injury and brain injury professionals are brilliant. Their story, as told here, is an inspiration to all.

Alexandria, Virginia
September, 1999

Acknowledgements

I want to thank my dearest friend, Kit Salisbury, who first read, edited and critiqued this book. She corrected the spelling errors, told me to toss one entire chapter, and fixed my split infinitives!

Thanks also to the unidentified publishing company who told my then agent, "She isn't Tolstoy," and then refused to purchase the manuscript.

And finally, thanks to my son David A. Bethune, who explained to me what I needed to do to be more like Tolstoy. David worked with me over a period of months from his home in Key West, Florida. I emailed chapters to him and he emailed back suggestions. He did the final editing and formatting of the book. He helped me greatly in arranging the material as both a story and a guide for families. I owe him a debt for his boundless enthusiasm and his technical brilliance.

Introduction

Writing this book caught me by surprise. I never expected to have the kind of overwhelming experience that warrants writing a book. That changed in August of 1994 when my younger son Michael was profoundly brain injured in a car accident. Suddenly, I was jerked into an unknown arena—one filled with fear and dread, surrounded by frightening medical procedures, equipment, hospitals, drugs, and surgery. Around every corner lurked the insurance company with its power to approve or deny.

Michael spent a total of 22 months in four different medical facilities. By that time, I had been transformed into a strong advocate for my son, a seasoned veteran of institutional behavior, and an insurance expert. Life had slammed me into a brick wall. I was exhausted, but somehow I was still standing.

In 1998, I decided that my experience and the conclusions I drew from it might help others who found themselves on the same terrifying journey. I spent the next six months drafting this text. As I read it now, I wish that someone had handed me a copy when my son was in Intensive Care ten years ago. What a difference it would have made!

This book is made up of two parts: Part One is the story of what happened to Michael and to our family. Part Two is a guide for families who are dealing with their own recovery from trauma.

If you are experiencing the traumatic injury of a loved one, know that my heart goes out to you in your quest to achieve the very best care and outcome possible.

1

The Phone Call

*A*ugust 20th, 1994 was a beautiful, hot Saturday afternoon. My son Michael and his friend Joe had gone to the beach on Highway 1, north of Santa Cruz. My husband was running an errand at the Long's drugstore a few miles from our house. It was a lazy day and I was lying on the bed in a pair of shorts and a T-shirt, reading the civil rights history *Eyes On The Prize*. At 2:30 PM, the phone rang. "This is Jane Tanner, a social worker with San José Medical Center. Are you Michael Grant Krizia's mother?"

"Yes."

"I'm very sorry to tell you that your son has been very seriously injured in a car accident."

Trying to take this in, I replied, "Is this some kind of a joke?"

"No, I'm sorry it isn't. You need to get someone to bring you over to the hospital. I don't want you to drive yourself."

She asked if I knew the name of the person in the car with Michael.

"Yes, Joe Lambinas."

Jane Tanner told me she was not sure who, but there had been a fatality.

As I hung up the phone, I heard my husband Marty coming through the front door. I hurried downstairs to tell him, then changed into a blouse and some tennis shoes for the forty-minute drive over the mountain into San José.

The trip to the hospital happened in slow motion. Marty and I said almost nothing to each other. We usually had the car radio on, but no one touched it. I wanted him to drive faster as I silently agonized over every bump, every turn, while Jane Tanner's grave manner reverberated through my head. Feeling terrific anxiety and barely able to remain seated, I tried to prepared myself to hear that Michael had died.

———————————

At twenty-two, Michael had found success as a cosmetologist. He graduated from Wayne's College of Beauty four years earlier as a part of a vocational program. He did not, however, initially believe that this training would result in his having to work.

Philosophically opposed to the fact that people have to have money, Michael experienced a series of adventures living on his own. These included a month of being homeless on the streets of Santa Cruz. Finally accepting that he had to function in the real world, Michael secured a position with a local hair salon and soon found a steady clientele. He was very talented and experimental with hair color and young women loved his work.

With the help of his biological father, Michael acquired a Volkswagen bus. With the help of his charm and good looks, he acquired a new boyfriend named Joe Lambinas. Joe was a positive influence on Michael, encouraging him to pay more attention to the tedious details and demands of life—paying parking tickets, and getting tune-ups on the bus.

Joe was 30 and had grown up in an extremely dysfunctional and abusive family. On one occasion, the children were forced to stay outside in very cold weather. Half of three fingers were missing on Joe's left hand, the result of a burn he sustained while helping his brothers and sisters build a fire outside.

Marty and I liked Joe a lot and in the early summer of 1994 we invited him to live in our house. Joe loved being part of our family and turned out to a very helpful housemate, often working with me in the kitchen or the yard. We enjoyed sharing our lives with these two young men.

I met my husband Marty while he was visiting an accounting client, the carpet warehouse where I worked in 1977. I was divorced at the time and my two sons were eight and five. Marty was 35 and had never been married. He owned his own home and seemed quite content with his single life. I found him handsome, calm, and sincere.

As we dated and got to know one another, I sensed a deep sadness in Marty. Perhaps it came from the loss of his mother to cancer when he was fourteen and the resulting stay with his inattentive, uncommunicative stepfather.

On a more superficial level, I observed that Marty ate out every meal. His kitchen cabinets held only bulky accounting ledgers and canned cat food. Typically the fridge would offer only a six-pack of beer and one of Coke. There were no pots or pans or basic cooking ingredients like flour and sugar.

I not only fell in love with Marty, I thought I could rescue him. I was certain my love and nurturing would add positively to his life. The first year that we dated, he came for dinner two nights a week. The second year, he came four nights a week and I started doing his laundry. By the third year, he was eating at my house every night. We married in June 1981.

Marty sold his house in San José and the four of us moved into a lovely split-level home in Scotts Valley. Marty was a self-employed accountant, the primary wage earner. I worked in an executive support position in the electronics industry, as I had for the previous few years.

There were lots of good times, especially during the first eight years of our marriage. I threw myself into domestic life. I cooked a sit-down dinner every night. I cleaned house regularly. I planted flowers, did the laundry, hosted holidays and birthday parties. I was juggling the family and a full-time job, but I felt content. It seemed I was managing.

We finally arrived at San José Medical Center, parking right across from the entrance to the Emergency

Department. My heart raced as we crossed the street. When the emergency department doors opened, a tall, slender brunette approached. Surprised at this personal greeting, I thought, This must be Jane Tanner.

"Jody?" she said. "Please come with me." She led us down a hallway, past several rows of people sitting in the ER lobby and a man lying on a gurney. Jane opened a door labeled Patient Consultation and ushered us in.

I hadn't spent a great amount of time in hospitals, but I immediately realized that Patient Consultation was a place of dread. A large, whitewashed room right off the ER reception, it had a solid wooden door, kept closed. An array of uniformly upholstered furniture and a few standard institutional landscape prints completed the décor. A telephone sat on the table next to me and bright florescent lights overhead. Being here signaled that this was extremely serious. We weren't going to have a conversation in the hall or the hospital lobby. I was gripped with fear.

Marty and I were both in the Patient Consultation room when I asked Jane Tanner if Michael were still alive. We were relieved to find out that he was.

Soon a handsome, youngish trauma surgeon, Dr. James Wyatt, came in to talk to us. He went over Michael's injuries, the most serious of which he said was a possible brain stem injury. Michael was unconscious. In addition, he had lung contusions and bleeding and a possible heart injury. Finally, he said, Michael had fractured his right femur at the hip joint.

Dr. Wyatt told us a neurosurgeon would soon arrive to implant an intracranial pressure monitor into

Michael's brain. He explained that this would allow them to monitor cerebral fluid pressure inside the skull. I asked about his chances for survival.

"About 50%," he offered.

Tanner told us that Michael would soon be coming down the hall after his CT scan and that we could step out and see him. I asked if he were cut or mangled. She responded that he was not.

Slightly relieved to hear this, I moved out into the hall. A minute later, a group of ER staff people came by with Michael on a gurney. He was fully dressed, and lying down on his back with his eyes closed. There were no obvious signs that he had been injured, save the rhythmic pumping of the manual respiratory bag that the nurse was squeezing. As he passed by, I reached out and touched his toe.

We went back to the Patient Consultation room. The waiting dragged on and on. I was anxious and needed to pee about every half hour. It gave me reason to leave the room. My body felt tight and my breath shallow. I seemed to be shaking inside. I tried to think clearly and remain calm.

I used the phone in the room to call Michael's father in Oklahoma and my parents in Scotts Valley. Michael's father had actually been the first family member to get the news from Jane Tanner. His phone number was the only one she could find in Michael's wallet. I flashed on the thought that I had often told both of my sons to carry ID and emergency information cards with my phone number.

For a number of years, I had battled the feeling that something terrible was going to happen to one of my sons. Knowing that I am not clairvoyant, I tried to dismiss it as something normal for a mother of two young men who drive cars and probably take chances. Despite my rationalizations, worry led me to take out a major medical policy on both of my sons about six months before Michael's accident.

Later in the afternoon, Michael's brother David and his partner Joe Rodriquez arrived at the hospital. David expressed what we were all feeling when he cried and said that he didn't want Michael to die without knowing how much he was loved. While we waited to hear that Michael was out of surgery, some dear long-time friends arrived to join the vigil. Talking with them helped us to pass the dreadful minutes and hours.

Eventually someone opened the door to tell us that Michael was out of surgery and we could see him in Intensive Care. It was after 10 PM in the deserted hospital when we rode an elevator up several stories and were brought into a large room directly across from the nursing station.

The room was starkly lit. There were two beds, but Michael was the only patient. His bed was on the left, surrounded by a frightening assembly of medical equipment. Michael was a body with tubes everywhere. His head had been shaved and sticking out of it was an ICP bolt—the pressure monitor with its tube and bag collecting red fluid. Another tube and bag arrangement jutted from Michael's chest. He was catheterized with a urine collection bag hanging from the bed rail.

A central IV line had been put into a primary vein near his neck. Both arms had intravenous tubes connected to bottles and bags. There was a ventilator with a mouthpiece taped around his mouth. Screens around the bed displayed his heart rate, oxygen saturation, and respiration. Michael was on life support, although no one said those words.

A nurse sat at one end of the bed. She looked so young. I wondered how she could possibly handle all of the assembled equipment. I was surprised when she told me she would be there all night. As we stood around the bed, she said softly to me, "you can hold him."

Much later I would realize the hospital staff did not expect Michael to live through the night. The nurse had gently indicated that we could—and should—say goodbye. I didn't pick up on the cue then, nor when Tanner told us the hospital had a house across the street where we could stay all night.

Even when the neurosurgeon, Dr. James Saadi, came into the room and, moving close to us, whispered, "It's very bad," I still had the 50% survival rate stuck in my mind. Though I didn't ask that night for a new evaluation, I later discovered Dr. Saadi told Jane Tanner that Michael had only a *five percent* chance of survival.

Despite the awesome terror and shock of these first few hours, I had a clear picture in my mind that Michael would live. I never really wavered from this belief, although it would be four long months before any medical professional would agree with me.

We declined the offer of the overnight house, opting to make the drive back to Scotts Valley. I felt I had to get back my safe, familiar environment. Knowing that I wouldn't be able to sleep, I asked the doctor for a sleeping pill prescription.

We left the hospital and found an all-night drugstore at the other end of San José. The pharmacy was at the back of the store and many people were in line waiting for prescriptions. As if in a trance, I made my way to the front of the line and said to the clerk, "My son has been in a terrible accident and may be dying and I simply can't wait in this line." She was very kind to put my prescription ahead of the others and I waited only about ten minutes. Marty and I drove home in a state of shock. I fed the dogs and put on a nightgown. Marty sat down on a chair in our bedroom and cried. Several times he asked, "Why did this have to happen?" We held each other. In the back of my mind I kept thinking that this must be a very bad dream that surely would go away.

2

Alive

I awoke from my pill-induced sleep sometime on Sunday morning, thinking Michael must still be alive because the hospital hadn't called. I got out of bed and robotically began my dressing routine. Everything was strange. I felt tense and anxious. I knew I was in the middle of a crisis and I sensed that I must take action, but what action? I have always been a "take charge" person, but now I didn't know how to do it.

I grew up in central Texas in a very traditional, conservative Southern Baptist family. We believed in the Government, the Doctor, and God. We did not believe in the chiropractor, the osteopath, or the psychologist.

Living as I had for a number of years in Santa Cruz changed my mind about many things. Santa Cruz, California is a diverse, very open community— a place where *someone* believes in and supports anything and everything. While living here, I became an animal rights activist and a vegetarian. I began to see a chiropractor regularly. I became comfortable with holistic medicine. Among friends, I counted Buddhists, Jews, socialists, gays and lesbians, atheists, political activists, environmental activists and an army of animal lovers.

By 1988, I was deeply committed to the animal rights movement, and in 1991 I took a position as the director of the Santa Cruz SPCA—the Society for the Prevention of Cruelty to Animals. The job was both extremely satisfying and excruciatingly demanding. With an executive salary came longer working hours, and I found myself with considerably less energy for home life.

In 1994, at the time of Michael's accident, I had been in the director's chair at the SPCA for three years. I was thirteen years into my second marriage and a few months away from my 50th birthday. Aside from the failed first marriage and the usual issues of raising two teenage boys, life had been smooth sailing.

After dressing to return to the hospital, I called my parents' house and found out that my cousins from San Carlos had just arrived. They made the two-hour trip after learning about Michael's accident. My parents live a couple of miles from me, and my husband Marty and I got in the car to go see them. We all met and hugged each other in the hallway. For the first time in my life, I saw my father cry. He said to me softly, "I wish it had been me."

Someone pushed a *Santa Cruz Sentinel* into my hand and pointed out an article about the accident. It was accompanied by a picture of my son on a gurney, being carried toward the waiting helicopter. I glanced at the story. It identified Michael as the driver and claimed that he wasn't driving safely. Unable to force myself to read, I put the newspaper down. Mom announced that she was going to the hospital with us—back over the hill to San José. My father, however, said he couldn't go.

Our family is a small one. Marty and I are only children, and both of his parents are dead. My parents moved to Santa Cruz County when they retired—Mom from teaching kindergarten and my father from his career as an insurance executive. My mom was always fond of bridge, often playing several times a week. Papa occupied his free time with watercolor painting, reading newspapers, and watching TV.

It would be four months before my father was able to go to the hospital. There were moments when I thought, hell, if the rest of us can stand it, why can't he? Intuitively, I knew why. He didn't have the physical or psychological hardiness to face it. My father always had trouble confronting difficult issues. His own alcoholic father was prone to fits of rage, and Bill learned early in life to stay in the background and avoid asking questions.

David and Joe, my mother, and Marty and I arrived at the ICU around ten. My mother burst into tears the moment she saw Michael surrounded by bloody collection bags and tubes. She was overwhelmed by the seriousness of the monitor screens all around him, the constant alarms sounding without explanation, the array of machines and IV poles that were to become the hallmarks of his stay in Intensive Care.

Joe, an especially kind and sensitive person, quickly moved to comfort her. We all gathered at the bed and stared at Michael, trying to take in the scene before us. I said to my mother, "As long as he's breathing, we have a chance," failing to note that a ventilator, not Michael, was doing the breathing.

We took turns in the room, standing or sitting around the bed, intently watching Michael and his equipment. At shift change, a new RN took her place at Michael's side to continue the hospital's round-the-clock, one-on-one vigil. After several hours, the shock of what we were going through began to take its toll and we staggered back to our homes.

On Monday, we were introduced to several other people who had been involved in Michael's case since he arrived at San José Medical Center. To make it to this second day, Michael had already needed a neurosurgeon, a cardiologist, a trauma surgeon, a lung surgeon, several respiratory therapists, a dietician, and a host of ICU nurses. These are the people who saved Michael's life in those first crucial hours, paving the way for what was ahead.

August 23, 1994

It has now been 72 hours since the accident. We just spoke with the cardiologist and fortu-

nately Michael's heart looks good. Yesterday there was concern about a heart murmur which could mean a mitral valve injury. Today's echocardiogram shows no valve damage, no blood around the heart, no heart muscle damage! Today his heart rate is much lower which is really good. The head injury remains our main concern.

David told one of the nurses that I'm a strong woman. I wonder if I am strong enough for all that is ahead, especially in light of my difficult job. I must find a way to hold it all together. David and Marty have been wonderful. We have some Xanax so we take one at night in order to sleep. It is the only peace I feel.

August 24, 1994

The hospital staff is terrific. I feel that Michael is in such excellent hands. We are fortunate.

David began immediately to ask questions about the equipment. Bright and technically oriented, he was able to quickly understand the machines and read the monitors. He had always had an interest in pharmaceuticals, so he also inquired about the intravenous drugs that the hospital was giving Michael and took notes in a small notebook.

When he found out the medical center had a library, he checked out books about head injury. David's search led him to be the first in the family to realize that, if Michael lived, he would be profoundly changed. When Dr. Saadi, the neurosurgeon who performed the crucial surgery that first night, was asked what we could expect if Michael lived, Saadi told David, "We don't know because people with this level of injury don't live." David began to gently pass this on to me, emerging as the family's first "information officer."

The hospital is another world with its own rules, most of them never communicated to the patient or the family. I eventually figured out that if I didn't ask, the doctor didn't tell. Later, as I became more skilled at asking, I would learn about the other end of the spectrum: asking and having them tell me about horrible probabilities. It seemed a delicate dance—the doctor wanting to tell just enough, yet waiting to see if the family asks for more. There was the question of how much truth I could bear.

The staff was beginning to nudge us closer to reality. On the fourth day, Carrie, the speech pathologist assigned by the hospital, introduced us to the Rancho Los Amigos Coma Scale. The scale, developed at the Rancho Los Amigos Hospital in southern California, is used throughout the United States as a system for rating the responsiveness of people in coma and measuring any changes they make. The scale runs from a high of 8 (nearly normal cognitive functioning) to a low of 1 (totally non-responsive).

Rancho Los Amigos Scale of Cognitive Functioning	
8.	Purposeful, appropriate. Alert, oriented. Recalls and integrates past events. Learns new activities.
7.	Automatic, appropriate. Robot-like appropriate behavior, minimal confusion, shallow recall. Poor insight into condition
6.	Confused, appropriate. Good directed behavior, needs cueing. Can relearn old skills. Serious memory problems
5.	Confused, inappropriate, non-agitated. Appears alert. Responds to commands. Distractible; does not concentrate on task. Agitated responses to external stimuli. Verbally appropriate. Does not learn new information.
4.	Confused, agitated. Heightened state of activity: confusion, disorientation, aggressive behavior. Unable to do self-care
3.	Localized response. Purposeful responses: may follow simple commands. May focus on presented object.
2.	Generalized response. Limited, inconsistent, non-purposeful responses, often to pain only
1.	No response. Unresponsive to any stimulus

Carrie informed us that speech pathologists were really therapists who specialized in cognitive rehabilitation. Speech was a part of her work, but she would also address such issues as memory, judgment, planning, organization, and self-control. Since Michael was at level 1 on the Rancho scale and a long way from speaking, planning, or exercising self-control, we didn't see much of Carrie for the next several months.

A week after the accident, I returned to work at the SPCA part time. The very supportive staff there was interested in Michael's condition and his progress, although people seemed unsure how or even *if* they should ask. I didn't want to make anyone uneasy, so I called a meeting to talk about the accident and explain Michael's condition. Several employees sat in the meeting and cried. I told the staff that they didn't need to ask me how Michael was doing every day. Instead, I would post updates on the bulletin board in the front office.

Michael spent two long weeks in the ICU, surrounded by machines and tubes and under the constant presence of a specialized trauma nurse—at a cost of $10,000 per day. The entire time he was unconscious, his condition extremely critical. He hung every moment on the verge of death-—relying on sophisticated equipment, delicate surgeries, and a dozen pharmaceuticals to stay alive.

From time to time, various members of the hospital staff would stand over the head of Michael's bed, loudly calling his name and saying, "Don't be afraid." Although I admired their advice, I wondered if he heard it, and if he did, how in the world could he be anything *but* afraid?

Michael's father, David Bethune, lives in Oolagah, Oklahoma. He flew to California and spent about four days visiting Michael in the ICU. In this first stage, all the family members seem compelled to be with their loved one as much as possible.

One family whom we met brought blankets and sleeping bags, staying at the hospital for days on end and sleeping in the ICU lobby. The irony of these scenes did not escape me… equipment, doctors, nurses, technicians, therapists, family, all on alert—and the patient completely unaware.

Our family began to discuss the idea of reaching Michael, even though he was unconscious. We decided to bring in a boom box and his favorite music, some Joni Mitchell CDs. I went through the closets at home and found a few books he loved as a child, and I brought these to the hospital so we could read them aloud.

During these first few days, several members of the hospital staff suggested that we try and get as much rest as possible. They told us there would be much to face in the days ahead. Of course, we were clueless about what they meant. Besides, we knew we couldn't possibly go home and *rest* when Michael was in such a desperate situation.

At this point, all of us were focused on him. We experienced a complete disconnect with the rest of the world. We stopped thinking about our jobs, our friends, and our problems. We forgot about food, about the lawn that needed cutting, the laundry and the bills. We were mental captives of the hospital and of Michael's tragic situation.

Even routine things became difficult. One morning, Marty let me out in front of the hospital and drove around the corner to park the car. He stormed into the ICU a few minutes later, asking for my keys. He said he had locked his in the car with the motor running!

I was lucky to have two caring neighbors, Denise Hite and Lori Joakimides, who brought over a dinner each night when I returned home from the hospital. I don't think I would have eaten if they hadn't cooked for me.

I was operating in a complete daze. I didn't *feel* hungry and thinking about food was just too much work. My friends simply showed up with meals and I undertook a mechanical process to eat them: put food on plate; open drawer to get fork; take plate to table; eat like a robot. I lost 10 pounds in the first two weeks.

One day I was buying a few groceries and I thought, "I'm here at Safeway and my son may be dying. This is absurd." I kept thinking that something about my emotional state must be visible to others, but no one ventured anything more than the usual, "Hi, how are you?" or "Have a nice day." I didn't know if I should say anything at all to people. What would I say? It obviously wasn't appropriate to tell the produce man that my son was in a coma, but part of me wanted to do just that.

Eventually I realized that, in the course of daily living, we must all encounter people who are dealing with their own extremely difficult issues, yet we're oblivious because their condition doesn't show. I decided to cut people some more slack. I have no idea what is going on in their lives.

3

Coma

August 31, 1994

Some of the recovery stages are pretty scary.

*I*n the upper left-hand corner of the Traffic Collision Report, a word is written in large, dark script: FATAL. The driver is identified as a white male, 22, Michael Grant Krizia. The car is a Ford Fiesta owned by one Heather Mazanek. Further down, a man named Joseph Kirk Lambinas is listed as the front-seat passenger. The handwritten note states that he died of multiple traumatic injuries.

A once-empty rectangle consumes the lower half of the Traffic Collision Report. In it, the officer has written his summary of the accident. The Ford was traveling north on Highway 1 at 55 miles per hour, approaching a Volvo that was stopped in the road. The Volvo was waiting to make a left-hand turn into a parking lot.

The Ford failed to observe that the Volvo had stopped in front. The Ford was forced into the right shoulder at the last second to avoid a rear-end collision with the Volvo. The driver of the Ford then lost control of the car on the uneven shoulder. The car spun out and wound up on the southbound lane, directly in front of a Jeep Cherokee. The Jeep attempted evasive action but could not avoid hitting the Ford. The occupants of the Jeep (a couple on their honeymoon) received minor injuries.

When Michael was about 15, he announced that he was going to begin using the last name Krizia. When I asked him why, he said he didn't want to use Bethune anymore. Bethune is my first husband's name, the boys' biological father.

When I asked Michael how he picked Krizia, he told me that there weren't any of them in the phone book. The family assumed this was a phase and life went on. Michael, however, was quite serious about the name change and succeeded in changing the name on his school records. On his own, he acquired other legal documents—a Social Security card and a California driver's license, in the name Michael Krizia.

In time, we all adjusted to the change. Our family seemed very modern; everyone had a different last name! Marty and I were the Paternities ("rhymes with *kitties*"). My older son was David Bethune. Michael was now a Krizia, and my parents were the Cramers.

Both of my children were maturing and growing into fine adult men. David had settled into a long-term relationship. Michael was working on a career in cosmetology. He had found in Joe a very positive influence in his life. Marty and I were finally past playing the role of active parents. We had enough money to live comfortably. It seemed that the future was ours.

———————

I was at the hospital with Michael when a staff member approached with a phone call for me. It was an officer of the California Highway Patrol wanting to ask some questions about the accident.

"When did you last see Michael and Joe?" he began.

"About 12:30 P.M.," I told him.

"Where were they going?"

"To the beach near Greyhound Rock. That's what they said."

The interrogation was shorter than I expected. He concluded it by asking if I would be willing to call the coroner because his office was having difficulty reaching any of Joe's next-of-kin.

I went home that evening and looked through some of the personal belongings Joe kept at our house. I didn't know any of his relatives myself, but I thought I might find someone who did. I came across a crumpled sheet of paper with some names and numbers. I recognized one of the names as a local woman named Leslie whom Joe had mentioned in conversation.

Struck with the difficulty of telling her that Joe had died, I took a moment to collect myself before dialing the number. After a few rings, a woman answered. "Is this Leslie speaking?" I asked.

"Yes…"

I took a deep breath. "I am a friend of Joe Lambinas. I'm so sorry to have to tell you that he has been killed in a car accident." She was silent for moment.

"Who are you and how do you know that?" she demanded. I explained that Michael and Joe were partners and that Joe had been living with us. As she learned the details, Leslie began to sob. I asked for her help in locating someone from Joe's family.

"I'll call Ray," she said.

Ray Rawls turned out to be Joe's half brother, though Joe had never mentioned him. After Leslie's call, Ray made arrangements to visit the morgue and identify the body.

Ray phoned other members of Joe's family, and soon his mother learned of his death. No one ever contacted me about holding a funeral, so I arranged an informal memorial service for him at the SPCA. We chose to have the service there in recognition of Joe's volunteer service. He was very fond of the shelter animals, especially the cats. My parents gave a $500 donation in his honor. During the ceremony, we dedicated a memorial plaque with Joe's name and hung it in the cat building.

A few of his friends attended the service. One brought a boom box and some music tapes. We played the music and offered a forum for people to share something about Joe. I had my comments written out in advance, but I was too distraught to read them, so a friend read them for me. I was filled with sadness that Joe had lost his life.

The Rancho Los Amigos coma scale became a fixation in my life and I listened intently to every word that the doctors or nurses had to say about it. I had always been afraid of the *idea* of a coma, although I had no direct experience with it. Somehow the word "unconscious" was less scary.

Dr. Saadi explained that Michael's "blown pupils" (fully-dilated eyes) along with decerebrate posturing (feet turning inward) were the clinical signs that Michael had suffered a severe head injury. For several days, Michael lay on his back in the ICU bed, his legs stretched out, feet turning inward.

I watched Michael lying there in a coma and I wondered if he could hear us. One day I arrived at the ICU to find him sitting up in a chair, his head falling forward. The nurse explained that it was important to get him in an upright position some of the time. Did he know he was sitting up?

A coma isn't anything like you see in movies and on TV. In the make-believe world, the person suddenly awakens, recognizes the people around her, and requests a spaghetti dinner. In the real world, any period of unconsciousness is a very serious medical event with potential long-term ramifications.

Many people are unconscious only a few hours and later regain full functioning. Others sustain a brain injury without ever losing consciousness-—football players, for example, who may endure multiple concussions.

For those in coma, though, hours of unconsciousness turn into days, and days into weeks and months.

The family waits in agony while, statistically, the prognosis for recovery becomes worse with each passing week.

When people do begin to come out of a coma, the process is most often gradual and painful. An eye may open. Later, a finger moves. The person may exhibit gross movements of their arms or legs, but he isn't considered out of coma until he can follow a simple verbal command like "Hold up two fingers," or "Squeeze my hand."

No one can tell when or *if* a coma will end. No one can tell what kind of damage a person will demonstrate if he emerges from a coma. But the longer its duration, the more likely it becomes that the family will face a very different person when their loved one awakens.

One morning Jane Tanner asked to speak to me. We sat down in a nearby consultation room around the corner from the ICU. She began by asking if I realized that Michael would be changed in some ways from this injury. I made some small indication of agreement but didn't ask her to elaborate. Tanner told me that families experience their own set of difficult reactions to trauma. She asked if I would like to talk with a hospital volunteer, the mother of a young head injury survivor. I jumped at the chance and a meeting was arranged for a few days later.

Tanner remarked that about 75% of families who experience a catastrophic event like Michael's accident don't stay together. She explained that this happens because the dynamics of the family change so significantly. I couldn't quite imagine what she was talking about, but I thought to myself that our family was special and surely would endure whatever was ahead. I was extraordinarily wrong.

———————

I met Maria on September 1st. She was a petite Hispanic woman who arrived in Michael's room wearing a floral print dress. I was impressed that she was giving her time to help families going through a brain injury. I hung on every word.

Maria's son, Robert, had fallen off a roof six years before. He was in a coma for two weeks and spent five months in the hospital. At the time of our meeting, he was almost fully recovered. Maria said she quit her job in order to be with Robert as much as possible. I thought, my God, I don't want to quit my job. Is that expected? I had waited my whole life for a job I truly loved and I wasn't anywhere near ready to leave it.

Maria told me that she used to go home from the hospital, step into the shower, turn on the water, and cry her eyes out. Although I didn't cry that much in the early days, I cried a river in the upcoming years and I often used her technique. It was good advice.

She also told me that Robert didn't want to go to physical therapy because it was too painful. He would shout at her, "Why are you letting them take me to PT!" She decided in order to deal with the agony of her son's pleas, she simply would not be around for PT. I also found this to be useful advice, especially in the early days, and I learned to let myself off the hook if things were too painful to watch.

The ventilator tubing went into Michael's mouth. It was secured with a wide strip of white tape which stuck to the facial hair that had begun to grow. A feeding tube went into one side of his nose and was also taped in place. It delivered a thick, gray substance directly into Michael's stomach-, the rate and amount of which were controlled by the kangaroo machine that was fixed to a pole next to the bed.

The kangaroo, the ventilator, the heart rate monitor, the oxygen saturation gadget, and the various IV lines all had independent alarms. Often, several would sound at once or in rapid sequence. It was unnerving since initially we couldn't figure out which machine was responsible and what each alarm meant. Looking at this intrusive array of medical devices, I knew that it must be terribly difficult to be connected to them—dependant on them. The nurses assured us that Michael felt nothing.

I was somewhat relieved when the hospital's trauma team decided that Michael should undergo a tracheotomy. A breathing tube would be placed into a surgical hole in his throat. At the same time, a gastrostomy would be performed, allowing a feeding tube to terminate directly in his stomach.

Once the trach was in place, someone from respiratory therapy would come by fairly often to suction the fluid from Michael's lungs. He would cough and cough, turning bright red. Even if he were in a coma, it was chilling sight to watch. Following Maria's advice, I left the room when a respiratory therapist arrived. One of them said to me, "He won't remember any of this." I thought, maybe not, but I will.

At home later that evening, it dawned on me: I had to face whatever my child had to face. I had to find the courage to look, to confront, to participate. The next time I arrived at the hospital parking lot, I began an internal dialogue. As I walked down the hall toward Michael's room, I would take deep breaths and reassure myself that I could manage whatever I would encounter behind the door.

I felt it was essential that I bring Michael positive energy. If I felt weak or shaky, I would wait a few minutes until I could collect myself. Often, I would call the hospital before I left the house so that I could get an updated report. Another strategy I used was to stop first at the nurses' station, look at the whiteboard to learn who was Michael's nurse, find that person and ask about him directly. That way, I was less likely to be surprised. Surprises in Michael's room were pretty scary.

September 2, 1994

Yesterday Dr. Saadi told David that Michael definitely has a brain stem injury and that he will have disabilities. It may be six months before we know fully his limitations. [It was two years.] The doctor said that the worst case scenario for Michael was that he wouldn't wake up, in which case, he'll die. In the best case he will have difficulty walking, impaired speech, significantly reduced intellectual ability and need assistance in living for the rest of his life. I feel very depressed about this news, especially in thinking about the possibility of his not progressing. Yesterday and today have been the hardest for me so far. Since I haven't traveled this road before, I'm not sure what to do. Logically I know that we must take it one day at a time and do everything to remain positive and hopeful.

After about three weeks in ICU Michael was moved to an area called "close observation" where he would have more supervision than in a private room, but less than in ICU. The close observation room was the size a two regular hospital rooms together. It was located on a different floor from ICU, at the end of a very long hall.

September 15, 1994

My mom and I spent about three hours with Michael yesterday in his new home in the "close observation room." I certainly see why they call it that because the room is small and everything is very tight. It makes ICU seems like a luxury hotel. In this room there are six patients and two nurses. Michael has been reunited with his original roommate, Mr. Suber, a 75 year old black man who rode his motorcycle without the helmet, hit the curb and has a brain injury. Both of them remain unconscious.

When we visit, we massage Michael's hands, feet and legs. We tell him over and over again not to be afraid and that there are many people to help him. His right eye is usually open and I have the definite feeling that he is looking at me. He will move his eye to the right or left side depending on where I am standing. Although his temperature is now normal, he perspires a lot, so we wipe his face while talking to him.

Michael exhibits "decerebrate posturing" which means his arms, legs and feet turn unnaturally inward. This is symptomatic of a severe brain injury.

One morning when my mother and I were at the hospital, we found Michael laying in bed, soaked with perspiration, his wet hair clinging to his forehead. He was running a temperature of 102°. We took a plastic dishpan that had been used for storage and went in search of the ice machine. After swiping two washcloths from the linen cart, we filled the pan with ice and a little water and began to wash Michael down with the frigid water and pieces of ice wrapped up in cloth.

In about 30 minutes, his temperature was down to 99°. We learned later that the temperature was caused by an infection, a constant source of problems during Michael's hospital stay. I learned that many people who initially survive trauma subsequently die of infection. On the way back to the car I said to my mother, "I don't think I can live through this."

From the very first moment the accident was discussed, Michael was indicated as the driver of the car. Santa Cruz District Attorney Art Danner even began a criminal action against Michael, charging him with vehicular manslaughter in the death of Joe Lambinas. Our family was devastated. Apparently, Michael was responsible for the death of someone about whom we cared deeply.

We wondered privately and aloud, how he could have missed seeing a car stopped in front of him? It was a clear, sunny day-—a straightaway on a two-lane road. We wondered if he and Joe were arguing. We wondered if he were fiddling with the stereo or searching for his sunglasses. It was a small relief to learn that San José Medical Center's toxicology report revealed no trace of alcohol or drugs in Michael's system.

I also wondered what would have happened if he had been driving his own VW bus instead of the tiny car he'd borrowed from a friend. Heather worked with Michael at the Jeanne Sumari Hair Salon in Capitola, another beach town just south of Santa Cruz. Before setting off on an extended vacation, she left Michael with the keys to her new Ford Fiesta. The Volkswagen bus was, of course, a much larger and more substantial vehicle. Had they chosen it that day, they might have been better protected from the impact. It was foolish to play these mind games, but I couldn't always stop myself.

Our family searched for answers. David researched the demographics of head injury and found that Michael almost perfectly fit the profile of the kind of person most likely to suffer a severe head injury: a male, 17-21 (Michael was 22), traveling on a Saturday or Sunday in a car on a two-lane road.

Trauma is the medical term for any kind of severe injury, including vehicle, bicycle, airplane, and boating accidents, burns, and falls. It also includes injuries to pedestrians and those which result from recreational activities such as climbing, skiing, or diving.

Trauma is killing our young people. According to the American Trauma Society, trauma is the leading cause of death among Americans under 45 and the fourth leading cause of death among Americans of all ages. This year, 100,000 Americans will lose their lives to trauma.

Every ten minutes of every day, 170 people experience a disabling traumatic injury. In 1989, a total of 58,000,000 life-changing injuries occurred in the United States, leaving 340,000 people permanently disabled and nearly 9,000,000 more temporarily so. Among youth 15 to 24, trauma claims more lives than all other causes combined. In 1990, trauma cost this country $173.8 billion in lost wages, medical expenses, insurance, and property damage.

September 16, 1994

Patty and I repositioned you in the bed, a constant challenge because the nature of the bed is to put you down in this "valley" in the middle. The bed has been terrific for your skin and it looks great, but it deserves a novel! The bed is composed of about 50 pillows which inflate and deflate on a rotational basis so that you are regularly turned in the bed. A number of people here know something about it (including David), but no one seems to have mastered the beast. Putting on the sheet is a two or three person operation and, if helping, it is imperative to get your side on first! Stretching the sheet across the bed and getting it "down" with the Velcro straps is similar to wrestling a python. As soon as one strap is attached, another one pops off. I have noted that, for the most part, everyone (including me) is satisfied with having the sheet sort of on.

Michael's unit was modeled on the Planetree concept. Originated at Kaiser hospitals, its cornerstone is the idea that families should be encouraged to take an active role in the patient's care, participating in their loved one's recovery as much as they are able. This concept worked well for us. In fact, I don't know what we would have done if we had not been allowed to be involved.

David quickly learned to work all the apparatus and could suction Michael or change the food bag on the kangaroo. We all learned how to position Michael in the bed. My mother and I became experts at dropping his temperature with the ice bath rub down. We called ourselves the "practical nursing team." We stayed in the room to talk to Michael and encourage him during painful physical therapy on his arms and legs. We struggled with the fancy computerized bed and changed his sheets. When we needed clean sheets, we went to the supply room and got them.

As I became more adjusted to Michael's condition, I was less fearful of opening the door to his room and confronting him. I gained more confidence about my ability to help him and deal with the equipment around him.

A normal human heart beats around 70 times per minute. We learned that Michael's heartbeat when he first arrived in the ER was around 200 beats per minute. Because of the extremely rapid rate, he had been "digitized," a special emergency procedure in which an electric current is passed through the heart to stop and start it again. Once we knew this, we found ourselves constantly watching the heart rate display on the ECG monitor. During good times, he'd be at 110 beats per minute. We remained concerned.

We also watched the oxygen saturation monitor which measured how effectively he was using oxygen. I observed that when I was near him, his heart rate went down and his oxygen saturation rate went up-—exactly what we wanted to see. It seemed that I had a special calming effect on Michael.

Eventually the doctors and the nursing staff took note of it, too. They began to ask me to accompany Michael during fearful or difficult procedures. The regular CT scans of his brain, for example, required that he hold absolutely still for 12 seconds. By himself, Michael would require sedation beforehand, but if I went with him, he didn't.

Dressed in a heavy, protective cloak, I would literally stand up against the machine, talking and touching him while his head lay in the tunnel that held the scanner. I was thrilled to have this positive effect on Michael, but it made me wish I could be with him constantly. Of course, that wasn't possible.

My own initial fear about being with Michael led me to know that visitors were also likely to feel apprehensive. In order to prepare them with some information before they entered the room, I developed a small flier titled *A Visitors Guide*. I mounted a cardboard box on the wall, just outside his door and placed a stack of guides in it.

The guide thanked people for visiting. It described Michael's injuries and the equipment one might expect to see in the room. It also explained his current neurological status and listed some things a person might do while she was visiting—play a favorite CD, talk to him about good times they had together, or show some of Michael's artwork and talk to him about it.

The brochure explained that Michael wasn't able to speak, but visitors would find a daybook on the table in Michael's room. The book had a bright, festive cover. Next to it was a canister of pens and a sign inviting anyone who came in the room to write a note to Michael. I wrote in the book mostly. David and Patty would write when they visited. Staff nurses and therapists left encouraging notes, too. When one of Michael's brain surgeries left half his head shaved and the other not, a young friend of his wrote, "Who does your hair?"

During the time Michael was at San José Medical Center, he constantly battled infections. He was plagued by repeated bladder infections and awful bouts with pneumonia. When his temperature was high, the doctor would say that he might have *sepsis*, a dangerous infection of the blood itself. He never did actually develop sepsis, but he did get MRSA, Mycellin-Resistant *Staphylococcus Aureus*. MRSA is an infection frequently picked up in hospitals, and Michael was a prime candidate with his already weakened condition and the lengthy period he'd spent lying down.

The presence of MRSA infection required that Michael be moved to isolation. He was immediately transferred to an empty room on a different floor in an otherwise unused area of the hospital. A warning sign was placed outside the door. It required that everyone going in wear a full protective gown and mask.

This was really hard for me. Not only was it uncomfortable, but it also worried me that we all wore masks. I wondered what Michael must have thought. Did we look like aliens? Would he recognize us? Did he think something terrible was wrong with him? Despite the problems associated with having to be "gowned," I found many things to like about the isolation room—among them that it was quiet, spacious, and private.

I wanted to find something that I could do while I was with Michael that might be stimulating to him. I came up with the idea of taking about six bottles of food flavorings to the hospital. I would open each bottle in turn and pass it under his nose. The staff told me he couldn't smell, but that didn't deter me.

September 17, 1994

I like the isolation room. It seems like a suite in an elegant hotel compared to the Close Observation unit. We have three chairs and a bulletin board! I put up pictures of Woody, Alice, Otis, Shirley and Patty and Papa. Your Lion King poster is on the wall at the foot of your bed. I brought a small pumpkin for your window. Today you responded again to smelling the almond flavoring. Of the six items I have for you to smell (lemon, peppermint, clove, cinnamon, vanilla and almond), you always respond to the almond by moving your mouth.

September 18, 1994

Marty and I went to the hospital yesterday. It is basically a daylong event. We stopped by Safeway and bought donuts to leave along with a thank you card for the ICU staff. Michael is moving more and more although it is not voluntary. He has some tremor, which is disturbing to see. He also perspires profusely which we are told often goes along with head injury. I look at him in the bed and my heart just breaks. I feel so badly for him. Occasionally out of his one open eye he has the look of sheer terror, sometimes sadness. His body is covered with the signs of numerous medical intrusions, a scar from a chest tube, a healing scab from his head wound, the tracheotomy and gastrostomy sites, mul-

tiple places where IV lines have been inserted. Such hell. When contemplating this and all that is ahead I feel a profound, pervasive sadness. I wonder how I will ever be happy again. I wonder if Michael will ever be happy again... if any of us will be happy again and how that will happen. Yesterday Marty and I read Michael's medical records and they are so frightening. Everything is listed as "severe traumatic." The opening sentence in the records reads, "This unfortunate young man..." I fear the future.

September 26, 1994

Last week's CT scan showed enlarged ventricles in Michael's brain due to fluid build up. Another CT scan is scheduled for Tuesday afternoon. If the build up has continued, Michael will undergo a surgical procedure called "ventriculostomy" where a catheter is threaded from the brain ventricles, down the neck, to the stomach for drainage purposes. Once in the abdominal cavity, the body absorbs the fluid. Of course, we hope that he will not have to undergo this surgery. On the other hand, if it will help, we feel fortunate that such a procedure can be done.

A month had passed since the accident and Michael remained in a coma. One of the most terrifying medical conditions is known as PVS, Persistent Vegetative State. PVS is what happens when someone doesn't come out of a coma. Infections claim the lives of many coma patients and most don't actually live for an extended period of time, but some unfortunate souls do.

I, like millions of other Americans, first heard of this condition when the story of Karen Ann Quinlan hit the media in the 1970's. Karen had mixed pills and alcohol and gone into a coma, remaining in a vegetative state for many years. Her family tried to gain the court's permission to withdraw all medical intervention and support so that she could die. In the end, they were successful, but Karen continued to breath after life support was disconnected and she remained in PVS for another 10 years until her death.

One day David told me that one of the doctors had said Michael was in PVS. My heart sank. It was a terrifying label. I couldn't imagine how we would deal with this and I struggled to find some conflicting opinion.

In the two month's since Michael's accident, I'd accumulated a collection of brochures from rehabilitation facilities specializing in brain injury. I started to call them and ask questions. At last, I found a rehabilitation hospital in Texas whose doctor told me that PVS should never be diagnosed until a full year had gone by. I had gotten a hold of something that I needed and I decided to believe it.

I also learned from David that a person is not in PVS if he can track a moving object with his eyes. Naturally, I became very tuned into watching Michael's eye movements and often I felt that he was tracking me. No official at the hospital, however, was willing to agree with me.

October 7, 1994

> *Yesterday my Mom and I observed that Michael was more awake and aware than at any time since the accident (seven weeks ago). For most of the three hours we were there he had both eyes open and responded to various hospital personnel and us by looking at us directly. He makes a number of facial expressions, all of them negative, but that is to be expected. I held the lemon flavoring under his mouth and he turned in the direction of the bottle. All "purposeful" responses are good. The neurosurgeon said, "He's coming around," and, of course, we hang on his every word. The shunt surgery is still not scheduled as he continues to run a temperature.*

Actually getting to talk to the doctor at all was much more difficult than I ever imagined. Dr. Saadi, a soft-spoken neurosurgeon from India, was, to us, a totally nocturnal creature. Sometimes he would come by to see Michael at two or three o'clock in the morning. He spent the days seeing patients in his office and our family often went months without being able to talk to him at all. David was sometimes successful in talking to Dr. Saadi on the phone.

Dr. Wrobleski, the pulmonary specialist, was the doctor we saw the most. He was a middle-aged, gentle man who assured us more than once that Michael's pulmonary problems were not his biggest concern. We were certainly grateful to talk to him, but he wasn't the neurologist.

October 11, 1994

Yesterday while we were at the hospital my mother and I had the good fortune to actually be in the room when one of Michael's doctors came in! He said Michael is probably five days away from being in condition for the shunt surgery. We were also able to talk with his physical and occupational therapists. We found out that he spends about 20 minutes a day sitting up on the edge of the bed. He can't be left in a chair because he has no head control and his head simply falls to his chin. The therapists feel that he is making good progress in responding to simple commands such as "open your eyes" or "open your hand." Once he is out of the acute section of the hospital and more medically stable, the therapy will increase in frequency and duration.

October 12, 1994

Michael is making neurological progress and showing signs of coming out of the coma! The doctor told us that he is a good candidate for rehab, which is the first positive thing they have said to us regarding the brain injury. He continues to have periods of significant agitation where he sweats and thrashes. He pulled out two IV lines yesterday. It is difficult to see him go through this, however, we understand that it is part of the process and may even get worse. As long as a family member is in the room, he is not restrained (the thinking is that we'll watch to see that he doesn't pull out any tubes or lines), but when we go, he is tied down.

October 13, 1994

David just called to say he had talked to Dr. Saadi and Michael is out of the coma! How I have waited to hear this! Tomorrow Michael is scheduled to have a ventriculostomy and Saadi says we should see more improvement in about a week. This is the best moment since the accident!

4

Mrs. Krizia

The driver's license in Michael's wallet identified him as Michael Grant Krizia. Since I was his mother, it was only natural for the hospital staff to refer to me as Mrs. Krizia.

Before long, I would actually respond when they said, "Mrs. Krizia." More than once I thought, How crazy it is that Krizia isn't Michael's name and it isn't mine, but now we both have it!

As I regained some equilibrium after the initial shock of the accident, I set out to formulate a "hospital strategy." I felt it could only help Michael if, as a family, we were considerate, grateful to the staff, and helpful whenever possible. I began by making an effort to get to know the people who worked with him. I would introduce myself to everyone (including the housekeeping staff) by simply saying, "Hello, I'm Jody, Michael's mother."

In addition to his daybook, I kept a separate small notebook in Michael's room for myself. I wrote down a description of each person with her job function and name. It turned out to be very important to understand the separate functions of each member of the staff. It doesn't do any good to ask the respiratory therapist about the feeding tube.

During our tenure at San José Medical Center, I figured out that hospitals post a schedule with the name of the nurse assigned to each patient. By glancing at the schedule board when I arrived, I could greet the duty nurse by name, even if I had never met her. At every visit, I felt it was important to offer a smile and thank each member of the staff personally for what he was doing for Michael.

In the two years I spent with Michael in hospitals, I encountered many opportunities to talk to the nursing staff. What I found was dismaying. In recent years, financial pressures have led hospitals to assign more patients to each nurse. One RN told me she no longer liked nursing because it didn't give her any time to spend with patients.

Watching the nursing staff month after month gave me great respect for them. They have a very difficult, labor-intensive job. Incredibly, nurses told me that many patients are openly hostile. Recognizing that Michael's life was literally in their hands, my family and I decided to be as supportive of the nursing staff as possible.

I often made a basket of cookies or fudge for Michael's staff which I would leave in the nurse's station during my visits. When we were ready to leave San José Medical Center, a nurse jokingly told me they were so used to getting goodies from us, they would have to organize their own refreshment program when we were gone.

I also wrote the occasional thank you note, or brought fresh flowers from the yard. I made an effort to get to know the staff while being sensitive to the fact that they were very busy and could not engage in long conversations with me.

———————————

As a child, Michael demonstrated considerable artistic ability. When he was a teenager, he spent a lot of time in his room working on art. Artists are not known for neatness, and eventually I had to give up on damage control. The damage was substantial: bedspreads, towels, clothing, carpets, and walls. Everything was an easel for Michael. The walls of his room were little more than Swiss cheese, so many holes had been made from posting his artwork.

Michael was a musician, too. He played the piano and enjoyed creating spontaneous compositions in his own new age musical style. He also wrote powerful, complex poetry that attempts to put into words his deep spiritual and romantic longings. Michael was a very private man and while quite expressive in his art, he didn't enjoy explaining his creations or his gifts.

About six or seven weeks after the accident, I had the idea of matting some of Michael's artwork and putting it up in the hospital room. Although he could draw and paint with exceptional realism, Michael preferred abstract, mysterious paintings, powerful in their use of bright colors, bold strokes, and ambiguous themes. I went through his portfolio and selected about four large pieces to take to the art store for matting. The salesperson there suggested I have them shrink-wrapped in plastic, which turned out to be an excellent idea. Each piece of art was protected and yet lightweight.

10-22-94

Today you really studied the two paintings we brought in. You looked at each of them for quite a long time. You are definitely connecting with them.

I found that hospitals are generally tolerant about putting things on the wall, much more so than I would have guessed. I was conscious of not wanting to put holes in the walls, so I used big strips of wide, clear packaging tape to mount Michael's artwork.

I also took advantage of bare wall space or bulletin boards to put up family pictures and get well cards. When a person is in a coma, it is impossible for the hospital staff to get to know him. I not only wanted Michael to be surrounded by familiar objects, but I wanted the staff to see that he was a very special individual. The strategy must have worked. We found this entry in his daybook from an occupational therapist.

October 26, 1994

Thank you so much for bringing in some of Michael's artwork. I took it off the wall and showed it to him and you should have seen his eyes brighten! I am especially appreciative for all the pictures and artwork you have shared for they help me to maintain perspective on what is really important... the <u>person</u> *behind the "patient."*

In another attempt to connect with Michael, I brought another visitor with me: Michael's wonderful, fat, fluffy cat, Kyle. Kyle was usually very calm and had a lot of self-confidence. He would sully up to a chair or couch and drape himself over your arm or leg, purring loudly. One morning, I put Kyle in the cat carrier and took him with me to the hospital. Since Michael didn't have a roommate, I didn't ask anyone's permission. As soon as I let Kyle out of the carrier, he hurried under the bed. Getting down on the floor, I coaxed him out several times and put him back on the bed with Michael.

Kyle would have none of it. He immediately got down and went back under the bed. Soon he began to howl! Michael seemed agitated and I certainly was, too. My visit was cut short by having to capture Kyle, struggle to get him into the carrier, and take him home. Kyle seemed pleased to be off the hospital visiting list.

———————

I worked half days for the second and third weeks after the accident. After that I worked a little more than 30 hours a week. I was very fortunate to have a position that allowed for this flexibility and, for the most part, I found it beneficial to go to work. It gave me something else to think about.

In time, I found I could actually go a little while without being consumed by thoughts of Michael and the accident. I don't know what would have happened if I had quit my job, but I think in retrospect that staying on was the right decision for me.

I dealt with some of my anxiety by calling the hospital, often as many as three or four times a day. I never detected any hint that the staff objected to my calls and their reassurances were a great help to me.

I always asked about Michael's temperature, knowing that an elevation in temperature likely signaled a new infection. I would ask if he seemed calm. When he didn't, the nursing staff would find a kind way to tell me, saying, "He had a rough afternoon."

Even though I was confident about San José Medical Center and especially the Planetree unit, I accepted the fact that no place is perfect. I felt that, unless I had significant grievances, Michael's needs would be better served by my remaining as positive and grateful as possible in front of the staff. In time, I would develop a well-defined plan for dealing with the less-than-perfect hospital.

By the first part of November, the social worker assigned to Michael's case was talking about moving him to a subacute facility. From discussions with the hospital discharge planner, I learned that a subacute facility is one which accepts patients who are basically medically stable, though far from well. A subacute may have full hospital accreditation, but in place of a full-time staff of doctors like you would find in a hospital, sub-acutes often use part-time doctors on scheduled visits.

Subacutes facilities have far more Certified Nursing Assistants (CNAs) than Registered Nurses (RNs), but this problem is not unique to subacutes. Across the medical industry, hospitals are replacing experienced staff with new workers in lower-paying positions. The result? Facilities cost less to operate and are more profitable for their owners.

For the first time since Michael entered the hospital, I became aware of the insurance company lurking in the background with its similar motivations. They wanted him to move to a less expensive facility as soon as possible.

All along, our family hoped that Michael could eventually be moved to Santa Cruz County, closer to home where we could see him more often. The discharge planner suggested several places we might visit.

Our first choice was Pacific Coast Manor, a sub-acute in Capitola, not far from home. My mother and I visited there and were impressed. We told the social worker that Michael could transfer there when he was ready. A bit discomfited to be leaving our now-familiar surroundings, we were relieved to find a good facility so close to home and elated that Michael was moving forward.

On November 28th, Pacific Coast Manor declined to accept Michael. We were told it was something about the number of beds. Next to decline admission was Los Gatos Community Hospital, citing his MRSA infection and a poor prognosis for brain injury recovery.

We had high hopes for Santa Clara Valley Medical Center. The county hospital for Silicon Valley, it's also the Regional Center for head injury with an excellent reputation in the field. I made an appointment with Diane Brown, an admission's coordinator there.

Diane asked me what I hoped would happen for Michael. I told her that I wanted to have a reliable way to communicate with him and I wanted him to have some kind of quality life. Mom and I toured the hospital unit where Michael would stay, noting quite a few empty beds. I was very hopeful, not only because of the empty beds, but also because Michael, unlike many Valley Med patients, came with the coveted Blue Cross card, evidence of his private insurance coverage. On December 11th, Valley Medical Center informed us that Michael had been denied.

As with all things in life, hospitals are political places. Subacute facilities maintain and publish outcome statistics, showing how many patients were able to return to their homes, how many returned to work, how many went to skilled nursing centers, how many died.

Naturally, public relations depend on a high percentage of patients being successfully reintegrated into the community, so before accepting a patient, subacutes and specialized care facilities consider the individual's potential for recovery. It appears that Valley Medical Center turned Michael down because of poor prognosis. I was simply devastated. In the meantime, the insurance company relentlessly continued their push on the hospital to have Michael leave.

The bend in Michael's legs was an issue. By the fourth day in ICU, his legs were rigidly bent at the knees and it was no longer possible to pull them down. The physical therapist explained that this contracture was caused by increased muscle tone, itself the result of the brain injury. At the time, we had no hint of the ultimate ramifications this would have. When a loved one is hanging between life and death, the fact that his legs are bent seems unimportant.

From time-to-time, the hospital would attempt to do something about it. They developed splints at the hospital lab and posted a schedule for Michael to wear them. He always seemed very agitated when the staff manipulated his legs or attempted to put on the splints. As a family, we hated to have Michael endure anything painful, so we didn't press for splints or a strict wearing schedule. After several months, a technician who worked for an outside firm was brought in to take a look at Michael and develop a leg-straightening contraption for him to wear.

November 5, 1994

P.T. just came in to work with you. You have a very hi-tech-looking pair of splints for your legs. It looks like you could walk on the moon in them!

In general, it seemed to us that all the varieties of splints and "shoes" were ineffective as they usually didn't fit or stay in position. Numerous revisions were made, each one adding new Velcro straps or new padding. The staff struggled with the issue of Michael's legs, failing to instill in us the confidence that they knew what they were doing. Even so, it wasn't a high priority item so we asked few questions.

Despite the team's efforts, Michael's legs remained bent with his feet turning inward. Common sense told us that the situation probably wasn't being handled correctly, but we had temporarily suspended common sense—a big mistake.

Almost four years later, I learned that Michael would have benefited from having a *physiatrist* on his case. We didn't have one because no one in the family had ever heard of a physiatrist. A physiatrist is a doctor of rehabilitation whose approach is typically more holistic than that of a specialist who looks mainly at one part of the body, like the brain or lungs.

A physiatrist is concerned about long-term, residual problems which are outside the domain of the acute care specialist. We know now what we didn't know then: decisions made today during the acute phase of hospitalization can hinder recovery tomorrow.

An insurance company made one of those crucial decisions. On the basis of their assertion that Michael was unlikely to live, aggressive treatment for his legs was denied. If we had been successful at getting a physiatrist on Michael's team, it seems likely the leg issue would have been addressed earlier, offering the potential for a substantially better outcome.

By mid-December, Michael had another infection. Dr. Wroblenski, his lung specialist, thought we should discuss whether we wanted to treat the infection, considering his neurological status. Basically, we were being asked if we wanted to let Michael die.

Michael's father and his grandmother Pearl were in town, so they joined David and Joe, my mother, and Marty and me for a family meeting. During the meeting, Dr. Saadi told us that one side of Michael's brain stem was now normal. He said that every patient should be allowed at least six months for evaluation—eight months in Michael's case. He had lost ground because of infections. As a result of the meeting, we decided to treat Michael, with one exception. Should he go into cardiac arrest, he would not be defibrillated.

December 12, 1994

I am depressed and tired and full of sadness. Yesterday the hospital put a "nasal horn" in one side of Michael's nose to suction him since they removed the trach. He hated the process of having the horn inserted and tears came to his eyes. I can hardly bear it that he has to lie in this bed and allow any and all atrocities to happen to him. I broke down for the first time and cried in front of him.

David took up the search for a subacute facility which would accept Michael and located one called St. Luke's Subacute Hospital in San Leandro, about an hour and twenty minutes north of our home. David, his father, and Pearl went to visit St. Lukes and several days later my mother and I did the same. The place felt very much like a nursing home, populated nearly exclusively with the elderly. After a quick walk around, I left my mother with the hospital director, went into the nearest bathroom, and cried.

A few days before Michael's scheduled transfer, we found out that he would have to undergo yet another brain surgery known as a ventriculoperitoneal shunt revision. The surgery, necessary to correct a valve in the shunt which had quit working, was scheduled for about 7:30 that same evening. Mother, Joe, and David were with me at the hospital when the news came.

At the appointed hour, a small team arrived to move Michael onto the gurney and accompany him to the operating room. None of us had eaten dinner, so we decided to walk across the street to a fast food chicken place. The restaurant was deserted, save for two customers. One of them was a man in a wheelchair. I looked at him and thought, I've never really given any consideration to people who are disabled. I was kind to them and respectful, of course. I did things like holding doors open, but I never took it any further than that. Suddenly, I was seeing the man in the wheelchair with new eyes. I made a point of saying something to both of them. We all said something to them. I realized that, because of Michael's accident, each of us would be more sensitive to the disabled.

Before Michael left San José Medical Center, Jane Tanner came by to say goodbye. I didn't see her, but she wrote in Michael's daybook on December 17, 1994

Dear Michael,

You do not know me yet! My name is Jane and I was the social worker on duty when you arrived here at this hospital. I spent time with your wonderfully loving family during those first few days. Their love, support and dedication to you and your recovery is and continues to be an inspiration to me personally and in my work with other families. I heard that you were leaving and I came to say goodbye to you and your family. I wanted to let David know that I thought of him quite a bit over the last few months as my sister died of a head injury in September. I thought about what he said to me that first night, that you were the most important person in his life. I worried that my sister might not have known that I felt the same way. So I want you to know this and when you recover, I hope that I can tell you how much your brother and your family loved and supported you here at the hospital.

Sincerely, Jane Tanner

5

St. Luke's

December 19, 1994

This was another in a series of unbelievably stressful, awful days. They just seem to top each other. At 12:30 P.M., the ambulance came to San José Medical Center to take Michael to St. Luke's. I rode in the back with Michael and felt a lot of motion sickness. Once at the hospital, I arranged Michael's room, talked with the staff, and spent the night on a cot next to Michael. He was very restless and I actually slept very little, probably due to the different bed. At noon today, Mom, Papa, Marty, David and Joe arrived and I went home. I've never in my life experienced the physical and mental fatigue I feel now. Time is a blur. My body hurts all over. I look at Michael's twisted body and half-shaved head and wonder how he and I will ever survive. I sometimes recently have had brief moments of wishing he had died, accompanied by a sense of guilt at my frustration and selfishness. Is it that I don't want him to suffer more, or that I don't want to? Both, I think. I must regain some balance in my life as I am about to spin out of control.

*M*oving to a new facility turned out to be very stressful. After four months at San José Medical Center, we felt practically at home. We knew the staff. We could find our way to the cafeteria, the various bathrooms, the linen cart, and the ice machine. We knew where to park and the fastest way to Michael's room. But moving represents progress, so it's an inevitable part of healing.

I updated the visitor's guide before Michael was transferred to St. Luke's, renaming it "A Guide To Working With Michael." The pamphlet briefly described Michael's pre-accident lifestyle and personality, the accident itself, and his injuries.

A major portion of the text centered on the topic of what could be expected of Michael's behavior. It described what caused agitation for him and what seemed to make him more comfortable. By this time, we had determined that Michael didn't do well with lots of commotion or talking in the room. Our realization fit in with what the doctors had said, that most people coming out of coma are easily over stimulated by too much light, noise, or activity.

The guide also gave the names of our family members and pets so that staff could use this information when talking to Michael. Michael's artwork, now matted and shrink-wrapped, went on the walls and ceiling of his room. Above the bed, I put a hand-lettered sign on hot pink copy paper. It read, "NEVER GIVE UP."

Although we really didn't intend to, we hit St. Luke's like a tornado. The staff was not used to such an involved family. These patients were elderly. Their families, if any, came to visit mostly on Sundays or holidays. A social worker there told me that about 40% of the patients didn't have anyone to visit them at all. Not only did we make frequent and unannounced weekday visits, we came with definite opinions about what was best for Michael-—right down to the type of diaper he should wear.

The hospital director, Brenda Liang, was a petite Filipino woman. She wore very smart, coordinated clothing with a bouncy, sharp hairstyle. When we asked, she graciously allowed David to conduct an in-service meeting for the staff so that they could learn more about Michael.

January 5, 1995 [by David]

Today is my day off from work, so I came to spend the day with you and to teach an in-service to the staff. Perhaps 30-35 people were there. We talked about three main ideas: good positioning to help get you in the best position to feel normal sensory input, good communication to help reduce the "whirlwind" of many types of stimulus at once, and being an advocate to help

*look out for your special needs and take action
for you. I got lots of positive feedback afterwards
and every one of your staff guides was snatched
up after I was finished.*

David and I both felt that having an opportunity
to speak with the entire staff about Michael was a good
thing. Those working with Michael indicated that it
was helpful.

It might seem surprising that the patient's family
would need to educate the medical staff, but it's especially important in the case of traumatic or long-term
injury. Family members have the best view of the "big
picture," the long-term needs and goals of the injured
person and his or her unique personality and experiences. Turning this information into active and positive input to the staff helps them to craft a more per-
sonalized approach to the person you love, which in
turn allows him to achieve his best possible outcome.

There are many types of head injury, but they can be
roughly divided into two kinds: open and closed. In an
open head injury, such as a gunshot wound, a specific
section of the brain is damaged. Often, injury is limited to individual impairments, like memory, speech,
or motor difficulties—but not all of these at once. The
same is true for stroke victims. Their injuries affect a
small, specific area of the brain.

Michael had survived a closed head injury, in which
the brain itself is subjected to massive acceleration and
deceleration forces as it moves inside the intact skull,
resisting the force of the impact with its own inertia,

then bouncing back-and-forth after the initial collision.

This bouncing and shaking tears the brain cells
themselves, resulting in a condition known as diffuse
axonal injury. Because the entire brain is involved, damage is spread throughout, affecting memory, speech,
motor, emotional, psychological, learning, judgment,
motivation, and other functions in interrelated ways
that make it impossible to predict outcome except in
very general terms.

Michael transferred to St. Luke's around December
20th, making the First Hospital Christmas even more
stressful. All the family was gathered together but,
neglecting to make any meal arrangements, we soon
found that virtually no restaurants were open. Mother,
Dad, Marty, Joe and I went to a truck stop to get some
hamburgers while David stayed at the hospital with
Michael. It was bleak. One bright spot was that Michael
went outside to sit in the sun for the first time since his
accident on August 20th. He wore his new blue sweat-
pants and a yellow shirt.

December 25, 1994

*Today Marty and I left Scotts Valley about
10:30 and we were at the hospital by 11:40 due to
the very light traffic. Joe, David, Mom and Papa
were already there. Michael was dressed and up
in a chair for part of the day. After opening presents in his room (he had presents, but couldn't
open any), Marty and Joe trimmed Michael's*

*beard. Then the guys gave him a bath. He looked
great! We are all so stressed out. I wonder how
long we can keep it up before one of us collapses
under the pressure.*

In Michael's hospital daybook I wrote:

*We're so thankful that you're alive and with
us.*

I came to realize that because various family members were at the hospital often and we had questions and concerns, we needed a point person—a hospital employee with decision-making authority who could work with us to resolve concerns. I spoke to Brenda about it. She thought it was a good idea and agreed that she would be the contact person.

We held a family conference and agreed that we would write down concerns and issues, including the day and time something happened and who was involved. The next family member to be at the hospital would ask for a meeting with Brenda to go over the issues.

Although this system didn't always work, I absolutely believe it is the right way to go. It is essential for the family to be organized enough to clearly articulate concerns, providing as much backup information as possible.

For example, patients in subacutes are often scheduled for physical, occupational or speech therapy in 30-minute sessions. All hospitals have printed copies of these schedules. Therapists, of course, can get behind schedule from meetings or other commitments that run late. Our family thought that these therapies were very important for Michael and we wanted him to receive the maximum amount.

It would not be beneficial for us simply to go to a meeting and say, "It doesn't seem like Michael gets as much therapy as other patients." We needed documentary evidence, so we asked for a copy of the schedule. We started paying attention to who was working with Michael and when, writing down the name of each therapist and the date and time of the sessions. This was something we could take to our hospital contact. Assuming responsibility in this way proved to be an essential ingredient in our success with all of these institutions.

Another thing that our family did in order to smooth relations with the hospital staff was to ask the point person about the facilities "Do's & Don'ts." Apparently few families ask this question, because the point person always seemed delighted that we cared enough to inquire.

At St. Luke's, we had a number of opportunities to work on a lesson that would become a constant theme: Everything Will Not Be Perfect. In order to live with the compromises inherent in the medical system, it was critical that we decide what was essential and practice letting go of the rest.

My mother, on one of her numerous shopping expeditions, found some wonderful soft pillows for Michael. She wrote his name on them with a permanent marker, took them to the hospital, and arranged them on Michael's bed. When she next went to look for them, the pillows were gone.

I could see how a pillow or two could easily disappear. Michael left St. Luke's periodically for CT scans, which were performed at a regular hospital. He would be transferred onto a gurney with a pillow. Several transfers, gurneys, and tables later, he would be returned—with pillow or without.

When Michael was first transferred, he hadn't had a regular bath in four months, only "bed baths." The staff immediately scheduled him for a bath. I watched in amazement as he was wheeled onto a platform that lifted his wheelchair into the air and down into a very deep tub. Michael didn't seem too pleased, but I thought the stimulation was good for him.

At St. Luke's, patients dress in regular street clothes. We had to make some fast moves to come up with comfortable clothing that Michael could wear in place of the hospital gowns he had worn up to now. The leg contractures continued, his feet were turned inward in a claw-like shape which made shoes out of the question. We settled on large sweat pants and big t-shirts. On his feet, Michael simply wore thick socks.

At San José Medical Center, our family had interacted with some therapists and we knew what they did. We knew that the speech person dealt with cognition in addition to speech. We knew that the physical therapist, the PT, dealt with moving the lower half of the body. At St. Luke's we were introduce to another therapist, the occupational therapist. Given Michael's cognitive state, the OT's work would focus on a set of basic life skills known as Activities of Daily Living. ADLs include things like brushing teeth, bathing, dressing, and toileting.

During our first week at St. Luke's, we had a family conference with the treatment staff. A representative of each discipline, a PT, an OT, and so on, reported on Michael's condition from his or her particular view. With her time, the speech pathologist introduced us to a new measurement, the Western Neuro Sensory Stimulation Profile, WNSSP. It had a maximum possible score of 113. Michael had scored 18 and was classified as slow to recover, typical of a severe closed head injury.

Much of the original research on brain injury was done with stroke victims. It was later determined that stroke patients actually recover much more rapidly than victims of closed head injury, probably due to the different effects of local and generalized brain damage. Because of this, new timetables and standard expectations have been recently developed for closed head injury survivors.

The St. Luke's speech pathologist had previous experience with slow-to-recover patients and felt very positive about Michael's potential for improvement. Physically, Michael couldn't do much more than lift one shoulder off the bed, or touch his hand to his head. He did not speak, or cry, or smile, or eat. He still had a feeding tube.

As Michael's recovery progressed, I became acutely aware that traditional medicine did not hold all of the answers. I was open to a friend's suggestion that I try Feldenkrias work, a movement system developed by

Russian physicist and educator, Dr. Moshe Feldenkrais. I had never worked with a Feldenkrias practitioner myself, but I knew that the process was non-invasive and wouldn't hurt Michael, and I was hungry for things that might help. Through a group known as the Feldenkrais Guild, I was able to locate a practitioner in Oakland named Rukmini Oribello who had experience working with a severely brain injured person. She suggested that we begin with four sessions per week.

Upon meeting Rukmini and seeing her with Michael, my father pronounced, "That woman is crazy." Though I didn't agree, I could see why he thought so. What Rukmini did to Michael was very subtle and difficult to describe… a little touch here, another there. Were we in for a surprise! After the first week, there was a remarkable change in him.

January 11, 1995

Rukmini has had a good week with Michael. He's now rolling on his side by himself! He also moved his head and looked to the right today. In addition, his WNSP score improved by 5 points!

Eventually my father would admit that Rukmini had helped Michael substantially. Her approach was to assure Michael that she would not hurt him. After all that he had gone through I imaged that he was delighted to hear this, if he understood. During the lessons she would gently suggest to Michael that he might want to try to sit up. She had a pole she would hold in front of him so that he could grab onto it and then she would gently pull him forward, if he showed signs of being okay with it. Once Michael learned how to do some movement, he did it over and over again himself as if he wanted to practice. He would spend hours lifting his shoulders off the bed in an attempt to sit without assistance.

Rukmini was into Ayurvedic medicine (which originated in India) and she wanted to try some of the techniques on Michael, namely using some aromatherapy. She asked me if I would pay for some high quality frankincense and jasmine oils. I agreed.

January 28, 1995

> *I am a stranger in this land so I often feel confused. I don't want to leave any stone unturned as we search for the very best for you.*

Rukmini would put a very small amount of the oils on Michael's clothing. She said that frankincense was used to bring people out of coma. I was skeptical, but open to different things. If someone had told me they knew of an Apache medicine man who could come to the hospital, start a bonfire in Michael's room, chant and dance about and help him, I would have said, "What's his number?" In looking back today, I'm glad that I explored a number of different ideas. I read Deepak Chopra, Andrew Weil, and Oliver Sacks. I read about the power of prayer and spontaneous healing. Exploration was a good fit with Michael's personality and style. It also helped me feel more hopeful, and hope is an essential ingredient for the family and the patient.

My father had not seen Michael at all since the accident. He visited for the first time on December 1994, making the trip to St. Luke's with my mother. When they returned, I asked him if Michael were better or worse than he expected. "Worse," he told me.

We decided as a family to develop a schedule for visiting Michael, to maximize our coverage. My parents went Sunday, got a motel room, and stayed until Tuesday. David and Joe came from San José every Thursday. I went to San Leandro and back every Wednesday afternoon, then again on Saturday with Marty. Michael had to be alone on Friday.

This schedule had very significant effect on my mother. She was then 76 years old and, though having lived many years in Los Angeles, she had never learned to drive the freeways. In LA, she and my father developed an elaborate routing plan that kept her solely on the surface streets. Whenever Mom needed to go somewhere she hadn't been before, my dad would map out a way to get there without using the freeways. Then they would take a test run together to make sure she could find the place.

By 1995, Papa was no longer driving and the only way my parents could get to San Leandro was for Mom to hit the freeways—difficult, traffic-laden freeways at that. I often felt like I was in the Daytona 500 on these expressways, especially as I got closer and closer to Oakland.

My parents' adventures in getting to San Leandro were definitely a team effort. My father functioned as navigator, watching for all changes of freeways and exits. The winter of 1995 was one of the wettest on record, hurling them with frequent bouts of fog and rain. One day my mother reported, "Two people shot me the finger, but I just kept going on." I was enormously proud of her for the courage she demonstrated in driving to San Leandro. We didn't know it then, but even more difficult driving feats would be expected of her in the future.

2-8-95

The traffic was horrendous this morning and it took 1 ½ hours to get here. I can't quite figure out the "best" travel time, but that's probably because there isn't any. Michael had arrived at St. Luke's with much more "stuff" than the average patient. Much of the collection consisted of things I had put together to try to "reach" Michael cognitively. I bought a group of paperback kids' books that had been his favorites when he was a child and he seemed to enjoy having me read them to him. Once in a while I even read them to some other adult patient! I also had the plastic box with "smelly things" in it. Early on we had brought a tape player and a dozen of Michael's favorite music tapes to the hospital. I also had

> *some items with various textures for him to feel*
> *such as sandpaper, a piece of fake fur, a round*
> *rubber ball, and a gourd with lots of warts.*

I didn't find the hospital staff very enthusiastic about these items or my "therapy," but I had to be proactive and find something to do with all the long hospital hours. I intuitively felt that interaction and stimulation were the right things for Michael.

As soon as his therapists would allow it, I brought bottles of tempera paint, big paintbrushes, and a large roll of white butcher's paper to St. Luke's Art seemed the best possible avenue to reach Michael, and I suggested to his therapists that they see what he might do with paint.

2-25-95

> *David was here Thursday and he reported*
> *that you used your paintbrush and paints while*
> *working with your occupational therapist. I'm so*
> *pleased that painting is being used in your ther-*
> *apy. Painting is so <u>you</u>!*

At St. Luke's, I also began the habit of taking Michael outside whenever possible. This presented somewhat of a physical struggle, as we had to be accompanied by a wheeled pole which held the feeding apparatus. It was difficult to maneuver the wheelchair with Michael and the feeding pole down the hall together, through the self-closing door to the outside. In my frustration, it occurred to me that few people must attempt these outings or better equipment would have been devised!

We went outside in all kinds of weather, including rain. Michael had always liked "weather" and I think that it was good for him to feel the rain on his face, or the cold wind. He was always appropriately dressed for the temperature. While outside, I picked pieces of vegetation for him to smell or brush across his cheek. I talked to him a lot about the season, the day of the week, or the time of day. I don't know what effect this had, but Michael continued to make improvements. By February 9, 1995, he was at 38 on the Western neurostim profile. By February 18, that score had improved to 57! On the Rancho scale, he was now a 3+.

3-9-95

It was pouring rain for my drive up this morning. Mother and Papa were still here so I saw them for about an hour. Right after they left the dermatologist arrived to check your skin rash and we had to put you back in bed. All of these adventures are so stressful on you and I hate it... sure you do, too!

I hate to admit that our family is human, but we are and at this point we're all pretty bedraggled and pooped. David quit his job recently so he's under that stress. Marty is deep into another tax season, one he began tired. I'm in the fight for my life at the shelter as four members of the board want to replace me because I am "too liberal" and "too nice to the staff." Patty has been on vigil with you more than any of us and she's pretty worn out. Papa has been her faithful companion. Anyway, we're a pretty sad little troop, but we're hanging in and we're so excited that you continue to improve. We all love you very much.

I was to continue my education at St. Luke's in Hospital and Insurance Politics. After four visits with Rukmini, Michael was demonstrating significantly improved mobility. He was now able to move his arms in all directions and sit up in bed! The family and staff were excited to see these changes.

Seeing the results in Michael for herself, a St. Luke's nurse asked Rukmimi to see another patient regarding Feldenkrais therapy. A few days later, Brenda announced that Rukmini could no longer continue seeing Michael. Her explanation, "She is taking too much credit for his improvement." I couldn't believe it! Who cares who gets credit? Michael was getting better. But the hospital prevailed. Because Rukmini was not on staff, St. Luke's was able to block her entry to the building, preventing her from visiting Michael or any other patient.

Another lesson featured Michael's severely contracted legs. The hospital suggested a process called serial casting, in which Michael's leg would be stretched and then cast in plaster for 10 days. With the cast removed, the leg would be stretched again and recast repeatedly until the doctor felt that the maximum amount of straightening had been achieved.

1-24-95

Belinda, the administrator at St. Luke's, called today to tell me they are ready to begin using nerve blocks and casts on Michael. Rukmini is really opposed to this so I've been talking to some physical therapy people who are also Feldenkrais practitioners and they are all inclined to go with giving Feldenkrais a chance and holding off on the casting.

David was also opposed to the casting. Part of my hesitation about it came from the fact that St. Luke's didn't have any experiencing doing this type of therapy. I told Belinda I wasn't ready to begin. She continued to bring it up from time-to-time, until eventually I heard from the case manager assigned to Michael by Blue Cross insurance. She basically said to me told me that if we were not going to authorize working on Michael's legs so that he could walk, then there is would be no reason for him to remain in a subacute hospital or an acute rehab.

By this time, I had learned enough to read between the lines. What she was really telling me was that Michael would soon be discharged to a nursing home regardless, as he wasn't showing enough neurological improvement for Blue Cross to justify keeping him in an expensive, specialized facility. Their contract specifically excludes what is known as "custodial care," so their financial involvement with Michael would come to an end.

The insurance company would pay for hospital time to work on his legs, but not for time to work on his brain. I realized that if I wanted Michael to stay in rehabilitation hospitals, I would have to agree to the casting. I insisted, however, that it be performed in a facility where it was routine. The Blue Cross case manager agreed with the understanding that I would soon locate such a facility.

One of the most difficult aspects of Michael's entire recovery was the battle with the insurance company. Over and over, I heard the same complaint from other families who were dealing with traumatic injury. Despite what the brochures say, your loved one must continue to make "progress" as they define it, or they no longer pay. Michael's policy made subtle reference to this when it stated, "benefits are provided only for the number of days required to treat the insured's illness or injury." Later, the booklet goes on:

> *The Blue Cross Utilization Review Program evaluates the medical need for hospital admissions and stays. This means that the hospital is medically necessary due to the kind of services you are receiving or the severity of your condition and that safe and adequate care cannot be received in a less intensified medical setting. If Blue Cross determines that a hospital stay or any other service is not medically necessary, you are responsible for payment of the charges for those services.*

This seems to be a universal insurance rule, regardless of the insuring company, and it translates into the fact that they will refuse to pay for continuing rehabilitation unless specific gains are proven by the facility or by a medical doctor, often by videotape. The courts have ruled that insurance companies only have to pay for those services which reduce the disability of the injured person and restore his functioning. Once the patient has plateaued or recovered as much as possible, insurance no longer has to pay.

I asked doctors, nurses, administrators and case managers, "How can Michael get better if he's in a facility where therapy isn't offered?" No answer was ever given. I felt afraid of the insurance company. It seemed like an ambiguous monster.

The monster reared its head over the issue of Michael's wheelchair. Hospitals have wheelchairs, of course, but they're generic and not designed specifically to accommodate a person with Michael's particular needs. The shape and size of seat cushions, leg, and backrests, for example, could be optimized for his posture and movements. As Michael would be expected to spend much of his waking life in this chair, these were important issues.

While at St. Luke's, his therapists worked diligently to acquire a unique chair for Michael, but Blue Cross would not agree to cover it. The policy excludes the cost of durable goods of any kind—physical medical devices which are not disposed of in use. This meant that Michael's wheelchair would have to come from Medicaid, an assistance program for low-income people. I didn't understand the system then and I still don't entirely, but I do know this: Medicaid never paid for a wheelchair. When we finally obtained the proper chair, it was funded by Michael's Medicare disability benefits in June of 1996, 22 months after the accident.

6

Kentfield Days

While we were at St. Luke's, Brenda suggested that I find out about the various services for the disabled in Santa Cruz County. This exploration led me to meet with a woman named Cheryl Bentley, the director of an organization known as Del Mar Caregivers. Cheryl's agency provides support for family members who are caring for a disabled loved one—Alzheimer's, stroke, and head injury victims.

Cheryl outlined the kinds of assistance for which Michael might be eligible. The list was daunting. It included Short Term Disability (SDI), Social Security Disability, Social Security Supplemental Insurance, and Medi-Cal, the state's version of Medicaid.

I didn't think that Michael would qualify for Short Term Disability but, at her urging, I went ahead and filed. It turns out that he did qualify for benefits, but because he was unable to endorse his checks, he couldn't collect any payments. After confirming several times that this was, indeed, the case, I contacted the office of our state assemblyman, Bruce McPherson. One of his aides was assigned to the problem and, after nine months, he successfully changed the law in California so that a parent or guardian could endorse SDI checks. I thought, Michael's accident has already done some good.

Gradually, I began to investigate the different types of benefits. Each one had its own process with endless repetitive forms, interviews at various locations, and documents that were required for each meeting. I came to believe that every applicant who was alive at the end of the process deserved whatever benefits he could get!

I slowly became more organized about the paper-work mess. I bought a black plastic portable file and set it up with Michael's driver's license, birth certificate, Social Security card and insurance cards. I carried this file into every appointment. Having it often meant that I didn't have to come back.

Later, I expanded the file by setting up folders for SDI, Social Security and Medi-Cal. I filed Michael's medical bills as they began to pour in. I clearly remember the first one. It was for the Calstar helicopter which had carried him from the scene of the accident to San José Medical Center on August 24th. The bill was for $10,000.

One of the services Del Mar offered was a support group for caregivers to brain-injured adults. Mother and I decided to go. Cheryl Bentley led the meeting and about five or six other caregivers were in attendance.

As we listened to people introduce themselves and tell a brief story about their circumstances, we realized that most of the families were five or more years beyond the injury. It gave me a big jolt of hope to simply see that these people were still alive!

These caregivers fascinated me. They got dressed and went to meetings. They laughed and told stories. One of them even had the energy to bake a dessert for the group. Another mother was getting ready to go on a Hawaiian vacation.

One woman had been taking care of her brain-injured son for 17 years. She reported that he refused to take a shower, "just sort of hung around," and would often experience grand mal seizures. I got the feeling that she would have preferred that he had died. Later, when I mentioned this to Cheryl Bentley, she replied matter-of-factly, "She may wish that." I felt that Cheryl was giving us permission to feel whatever we felt. Sometimes I wondered what I would think 17 years after Michael's accident.

I met Crystal Dunniway at the caregivers meeting that night. Her daughter, Michelle, had suffered a severe closed head injury as the result of a car accident in November, 1994. Michelle, a student at UC Santa Cruz, pulled out in front of a truck and was hit head-on. She was 20 years old.

2-20-95

This morning I went to Pacific Coast Manor to visit Michelle Dunniway. She's not as far along as Michael, but then she's only three months post trauma and he's six. She does not have the contracted knees that Michael has, or a shunt.

Crystal and I were both beginning a phase in our kids' recoveries where we were thinking about getting them into acute rehabilitation hospitals. An acute rehabilitation hospital accepts patients who are medically stable and who are able to participate in rather extensive therapy each day. For brain-injury survivors the accepted patient usually needs to be a level 4 on the Rancho Scale. Michael was approaching level 4 and I was anxious for him to move onto a facility that specialized in rehabilitation. St. Luke's lobbied hard for us to keep Michael there. Since he had private insurance, he was a profitable patient. We were told that they did rehabilitation, but I wanted Michael in a facility where they regularly and routinely worked with brain-injured people. Gleaning information from people at the support group I came up with a list of questions to ask facilities such as how many brain-injured patients do you currently have; how many have you had in the last year; what was their Rancho level when they arrived; how long were they here; what was their Rancho level when they left.

Crystal and I got the names of two possible facilities from the support group and we set out to visit them. We went together to R. K. Davies, a very large urban hospital in downtown San Francisco. The facilities were impressive with a huge gym, swimming pool and a "day room" with spectacular views of the city. At

Davies I saw an "optima" bed for the first time in my life. The bed was completely enclosed in a heavy blue netting so that the patient has free movement within the bed, but can't get out of it.

My mom and I visited Kentfield Rehabilitation Hospital in Marin County. We had a tour and then waited in the lobby to meet the medical director, Dr. Deborah Doherty. While we were waiting we saw a very attractive, small woman wearing a white lab coat. She had long brunette hair. She smiled at me as she passed back and forth through the lobby several times. My mom and I were soon to learn that this was Dr. Doherty.

March 5, 1995

Friday Mother and I went to visit Kentfield which is just north of Sausalito. It is a 60-bed facility in a very nice area of Marin County. This is the first rehab center I have visited which specialized in traumatic head injury patients. I was impressed with the doctor and the staff. I want Michael to go there. Tomorrow they are supposed to visit him for an assessment. It will take two hours to get there, but the commuting is less important than having him in the very best facility.

I am again feeling the tremendous background anxiety. Sometimes I can hardly concentrate at work and I feel fidgety.

Kavie Von Husen from Kentfield came to evaluate Michael. She took one look at his legs and said, "Poor guy, they let him get all contracted."

March 7, 1995

We're getting closer to having Michael admitted to Kentfield. The facility has accepted him and, so far, the insurance company has been positive. Hopefully he'll be transferred Thursday.

On 3-10-95 Mellisa Ridge, the social worker at St. Lukes wrote in Michael's daybook.

When you first came I could not tell what kind of personality you had. Now we know you are warm, you like music, you are playful, you don't like phoniness, you are determined and brave and don't give up. Maybe because you don't talk, it seems like you are the only person who is always being himself. That is what I am going to miss.

March 17, 1995

On March 15, his 23rd birthday, Michael was transferred from St. Luke's to Kentfield. Michael made the transfer in a van which takes people in wheelchairs. David followed in his car. I was behind with Michael's gear in my truck. Transfers are hell . . . so much to communicate about Mi-

chael to the new people . . . so much to go through to get the right equipment. Kentfield immediately ordered Michael an optima net bed and he had it Thursday morning. They seem to get things done much more efficiently and quickly than St. Lukes.

Michelle Dunniway was transferred to Kentfield also on March 15. She is significantly less awake than Michael. After the arduous transfer day I had dinner with her mother, Crystal, and her friend, Erlene. I made arrangements to stay at the Corte Madera Inn when I visit Michael. Their regular rate is $91.00, but I talked to the sales manager and told them someone from the family would stay four nights a week so she gave me a rate of $55.00.

Once again I updated the "Guide To Working With Michael" and set up a small box with the folded brochures on a table right inside his room. I brought way too much stuff to Kentfield and I collected even more as I was there. My philosophy about this was that I wanted to be comfortable while I was there. I also wanted to be purposeful and productive. Finally, I wanted to interact positively with Michael. I found that I needed many things in order to accomplish these three goals.

By now the shrink-wrapped art collection had grown to about 10 pieces and they all went up on the walls and ceiling. The pink "Never Give Up" sign went up above the bed. I brought some photo albums from home and left them in Michael's room so that the staff could see pictures of Michael before the accident. Also, Michael enjoyed looking at the albums. Our family made Kentfield history by being the first family to bring our own chairs. Early on I had learned that hospitals have a shortage of chairs so I bought two wooden folding ones that we left at the various hospitals.

On the day of Michael's admission to Kentfield, Dr. Doherty, conducted an evaluation of him. She wrote about that examination, "The patient is awake and alert. He tracks this examiner as I move around the room, though he does not sustain eye contact at all towards his right. He is unable to follow any verbal commands. He is able to try and cooperate when hand over hand guiding and gesturing with environmental contextual cues is available. He is able to take a comb and attempt to comb his hair when this is offered to him from his left side. He makes no attempt to take the comb when the comb is offered from his right side. He has no spontaneous speech. He is unable to answer yes/ no questions and makes no effort to do so. He exhibits a high degree of motor restlessness and rocks back and forth, and attempts to roll from side to side during the examination. He often grabs the examiner or his mother with one or both arms. The patient appeared fearful and anxious during my examination." Doherty estimated that Michael would be at Kentfield for four months.

Kentfield is an impressive facility. It is one-story and has three units, each with about 10 rooms. Michael was assigned to unit three which was at the back of the facility. The hospital has a small cafeteria, a comfortable family day room, laundry facilities (here the family is asked to take care of the laundry, if at all possible), a terrific gymnasium and a bright multipurpose room which was used for art therapy. The hospital is located adjacent to the College of Marin and a very nice path leads one direction from the hospital to the college and the other direction to the small town of Ross. Along the pathways strollers would encounter wildlife such as egrets which frequented a culvert, daffodils in the right time of year, tennis courts and players, bicyclists, kids, dogs and others in wheelchairs.

At the time of Michael's admission, unit three had mostly young and middle-aged patients. The staff was by and large young and enthusiastic and it didn't feel like a nursing home. In the nine months that Michael was at Kentfield he moved to four different rooms. Because I had so much stuff and because Michael was required to move periodically, I found it helpful to put a temporary label on the outside of the drawer or closet listing what was inside.

Every morning each patient's therapy schedule was posted in his or her room. I thought this protocol was impressive and hadn't seen it in any other hospital. My routine was to go to Kentfield every Friday morning, stay in the motel Friday night, visit Michael on Saturday and head for home around 3 PM. After arriving and saying hello to Michael my next activity was to check his therapy schedule so that I could plan my day. I usually went to therapy with Michael, often taking along my camera, my daybook so I could document the activities and one of our folding chairs.

Each day Monday through Saturday Michael would spend time in physical, occupational and speech therapy. Physical therapy worked on his feet and legs and such skills as standing and gaining leg strength. While in the gym the therapist would sometimes fold his body over a very large, firm ball. Sometimes they would strap him into a moveable table. Initially he would be lying down but slowly the therapist would move the table so that he was in an upright position. Sometimes he practiced using a battery-operated wheelchair. By the way, he was a terrible driver!

Occupational therapists worked on the activities of daily living such as tooth brushing, dressing, toileting, grooming and physical concerns associated with the upper body. Like others who have been in a significant coma, Michael had to relearn to do everything. When he was learning to dress himself, the therapist would hold up two shirts and ask Michael which one he would like to wear that day. If it were offered, he would always choose a tie-dyed t-shirt. Then the therapist would coach him through putting the garment over his head and getting his arms in the armholes. Michael had three severely contracted fingers on his left hand and this issue also fell under the purview of occupational therapy.

The speech therapist worked on speaking, memory, planning, problem solving, writing, organization, and a whole host of cognitive skills. Many times this therapy came in the form of playing games with Michael.

I learned a great deal by accompanying Michael to therapy. Probably the most important thing I learned was that, to some extent, I could emulate the therapy and possibly help Michael even more. I certainly wasn't confident about physical things, but I could often copy the cognitive exercises.

March 26, 1995

The therapist, Ruth, drew a circle and then asked Michael to draw one. He did a really good job! He also put on his sunglasses and showed what one does with a hairbrush and a toothbrush. While I was there, we took a walk along the bicycle trail and Michael really listened to the sound of water from a little stream near the hospital. He also played his keyboard.

Just five days after Michael entered Kentfield the serial casting began with only one leg because Michael's heart rate was high indicating that he was too stressed to do both.

March 23, 1995

The serial casting did not go well. At 11:00 P.M. I had a call from Kentfield that Michael was going to Marin General because his heart rate was at 160. I called Mother (she and Papa were at the Corte Madera Inn) and she got up and got dressed and got the motel van to take her to the hospital. She stayed until 6:00 A.M. and David arrived at 8:30. Tests showed that Michael might have had a gallstone and Dr. Doherty thinks his problems were not related to the casting. Nevertheless, she had the cast removed at the hospital.

A few days later I agreed to another try at the serial casting, but it wasn't an easy decision, especially since David didn't support it.

March 28, 1995

Today Michael had the casting done again on both legs. I hate, hate, hate it that Michael has to go through more terrible medical processes. During the procedures his heart rate went up to 160, but Dr. Doherty gave him some medication and by 7:30 P.M. it was down to 84. He also got some pain medication. I hope he'll sleep tonight and that we make it through this casting.

7

Family Matters

*I*nitially, everyone in the family was simply a grateful vessel – receiving information from the doctors, listening, and trying to comprehend. It takes time and experience to get to the point where the family might question treatment options, or where dissatisfaction with the facility and staff sets in. We were probably very typical in that regard, basically satisfied and compliant during the acute hospital portion of Michael's treatment. But as time passed we had disagreements among ourselves as to the best course of action.

Each of us settled into having our own special areas of interest and at times we were frustrated and irritated when others in the family didn't share our concerns. My mother was the comfort expert. She was constantly tuned into things such as Michael's dry skin and the position of buttons, snaps and zippers which might poke or snag him. She massaged his ravaged body, always on the lookout for rashes, blisters or pressure sores. She advised the rest of us to cut Michael's nails, put cream on his hands and feet, and be sure his room was at a comfortable temperature.

David was the drug expert. He had read enough to know that many of the drugs Michael took to avoid seizures and combat contractures also interfered with his cognitive progress. David told me that Michael needed to be off all drugs as soon as possible. He strongly lobbied the family and the doctors for support.

I became the designated brain. In this role, I tried to keep everything harmonious within the family and keep the family within the good graces of the hospital staff. I also dealt with the politics of the hospital and the insurance company and served as the final decision maker regarding Michael's care. It was an ominous responsibility and one which weighed heavily upon me, especially when we didn't agree as a family upon a course of action.

In reflecting on this, I realize having a designated brain is critical for interacting successfully with the hospital – someone logical, reasonable, organized, and responsible to represent the family. If this doesn't happen, you may be perceived as flaky, overly demanding, or just a bunch of time-wasting complainers. In other words, a problem family. Once labeled this way by the staff, how can you expect prompt, compassionate, and professional attention for your loved one?

For those who don't have a designated brain in the immediate family, I recommend looking to your extended family. There might be an aunt, cousin or uncle who would be able to fill this capacity, or even a close family friend. The designated brain will need to attend team meetings with the hospital staff to help relatives sort items into the "important" and "unimportant" categories and to provide input to the decision-making process. The designated brain might also help establish a visiting schedule or educate family members on appropriate visiting behavior.

In my capacity as the family head, I had to deal with calls from hospital administrators about the behavior of my relatives. I often felt like a parent getting a call from the school principal.

February 28, 1995

Belinda has called me twice recently to complain about Mom and David. I am too out of it to tackle it and I don't know what to do. I feel a storm brewing. What an absolutely dreadful time this has been.

March 1, 1995

At noon we had a family conference at St. Lukes. David declined to go to the meeting. It is obvious the staff is fearful of him. Belinda told me David had been rude to her again yesterday and said, "Don't try to screw me." I am so mortified by all of this. I believe I'm not responsible for David or my mother, but it is really hard to not feel effected.

Whatever David and my mother did at the hospital, I felt they acted only out of concern for Michael. During much of his stay, my mother was on duty, spending more hours at the hospital than anyone else in the family and nearly all of them at his bedside. My father went with her frequently, telling her, "I'll sit in the lobby." My mother saw more of the hospital's imperfections than any of us. She might sit by the bed for an hour or even two, waiting for Michael's tube feeding to be started. At some point she would become irritated, her feelings reflected in the edge in her voice. The hospital staff complained to me that she was sometimes harsh and demanding in her requests.

Their comments about David centered around the fact he is strong-willed, articulate and intimidating. He is also bright, charming, and witty. Because David was so quick to pick up on hospital jargon like drug names and equipment functions, the staff often assumed he was studying medicine. He would ask probing questions and understood their highly technical answers, a quality the team admired. But the other side of this approach required that his concerns be taken seriously. When he had a question, David wanted an answer; he is not an easy person to brush-off. If he wanted to see a doctor or speak with the hospital director and she was not available, he might simply go to her office and announce, "I'll wait here until I see the doctor." A nurse at Kentfield told me she had rarely seen Dr. Doherty intimidated but David had done it!

It is a tough situation for everyone. An emotionally drained family seemingly pitted against an inevitably overworked and often underpaid hospital staff. Can the family be perpetually polite and patient? No, and it isn't even a good idea to attempt it. Can the hospital be perpetually efficient and competent? No, in a long-term hospital stay the goal is to achieve polite, productive communication with the hospital staff *most of the time. Just as there is no perfect family, there is no such thing as a perfect staff or perfect hospital.*

In the first months after Michael's accident, my husband Marty and I worked hard at supporting each other. We cried together. We went to the hospital together. We held hands and were physically present for one another. Michael was the only topic we discussed. More than once, Marty told me how devastated he was by the accident. I never questioned his love, his concern, or his compassion for Michael but regrettably, Marty isn't psychologically strong to begin with. Soon the strain began to show. When Michael moved to St. Luke's in San Leandro, our commute time to the hospital doubled.

December 26, 1994

Marty is exhausted and stayed in bed most of the day. I'm worried about him.

January 1, 1995

I went to see Michael alone yesterday since Marty has a cold.

January 18, 1995

I went to the hospital alone today.

February 8, 1995

I went to the hospital alone today and it was a good day.

February 11, 1995

I went to the hospital yesterday, but Marty had to work since it's the tax season.

When Michael moved to Kentfield in Marin County, he was even further from our home. It was so far, in fact, that I didn't feel I had the energy to drive up and back in one day. Marty was making the trip with me less often than ever, resulting in a long period of spending nights alone in a motel room. He openly expressed concern about not accompanying me, often saying, "I just can't do it. I don't know how you do…" I don't know how I did it either, except that I am a person with considerable stamina. Despite the increased difficulty of going it alone, I was determined to continue to see my son, to be near him and actively participate in his recovery.

April 21, 1995

Today Marty finally came to Kentfield after five weeks without seeing you. He was able to meet many of the people who work with you.

I had talked Marty into taking a week's vacation in June to visit Marin County, home to Kentfield and across the bay from San Francisco. Marty always needed considerable time to recover from the annual tax season, but I thought that by May he would be feeling pretty good. The idea was to check into the Corte Madera Inn, stop by Kentfield for a short visit with Michael each day, and then take advantage of the wonderful tourist activities in and around the city. I drove up on May 5th. Marty was to come on the 6th. Instead, he called me and said, "I need more time here," agreeing to be in Marin the next day before noon. He showed up about 4:00 P.M. in a very bad mood.

May 13, 1995

The vacation was basically a bust. Marty was tired. I should not have assumed we could have fun. Guess we're not ready yet. Our relationship is in another slump. It seems Marty attributes most of his problems and tribulations to his association with my problematic family and me. At times like these I feel like separating so I won't be the focus of blame. I believe the biggest problem is Marty's refusal to take responsibility for his own behavior. I am also very frustrated and concerned about the fact that I can't tell him what I'm feeling without his becoming enraged. Sometimes he scares me.

On a typical Kentfield weekend, I would leave Scotts Valley around 8:00 A.M. on Friday, stopping at our local Safeway to pick up a roll, a bottle of orange juice, some peeled baby carrots or maybe a banana. Traffic was generally moderate and lighter after 9:00 AM when I could legally drive in the carpool lane. Normally a very conservative driver, I drove 70 mph most of the way.

The trip up the Junípero Serra Freeway took an hour and forty-five minutes. Soon I had memorized the details of this curvy stretch of road, dubbed "The World's Most Beautiful Freeway." Once through San José, the countryside turns to rolling hills dotted with cows and equestrian centers. I would pass the exit for Stanford University, named for the banker philanthropist who first endowed it. Further along the road, I could see the Linear Accelerator complex, a vast, long building stretching for 2 miles in a perfectly straight line that passed underneath the freeway.

I drove past the exit signs for the wealthy communities of Palo Alto and Hillsdale to enter San Francisco a few minutes later on 19th Avenue. The drive through this part of the city took about 30 minutes. I would think to myself, What is it like to live here? I enjoyed seeing the Painted Ladies, the rows of Victorian houses with their gingerbread architecture. I admired the diversity of San Francisco's population and the grand vistas of its streets going uphill on one side of the road and downhill on the other. Sometimes the city is shrouded in fog. Because of the way the road is designed, drivers on 19th Avenue go around a curve to find themselves suddenly face-to-face with the enormous Golden Gate Bridge in its magnificent International Orange paint, a sight I always find thrilling.

Usually I arrived at Kentfield by 11:00 A.M and stayed until about 6:00 P.M. when I would leave to get something to eat. I would often stop at a local grocery store and select something from the deli before checking-in to my motel room. If I weren't absolutely exhausted, I'd go back to the hospital for several hours.

The next morning I was up by 8:00 A.M. I'd go to the Corte Madera Safeway and buy a blueberry muffin, some fruit, and something to drink before driving the 5 minutes from the motel to Kentfield. I had so little time with Michael during these weekends, I wasn't comfortable spending it eating out. I solved this problem by snacking instead of eating formal meals. I would leave the hospital about 3:00 P.M. to be home in Scotts Valley by 5, where I would stop at another deli and get dinner for Marty and myself.

The routine was hard on both of us. Marty didn't cook or grocery shop and he never had a meal ready when I arrived home. I would consistently be tired and often depressed. I didn't make wonderful meals. I didn't provide sparkling conversation, and I certainly didn't have the interest or energy to be sexually alluring. I knew in my heart that this wasn't what Marty had signed up for in a marriage, but perhaps the worst part was that there wasn't any end in sight.

May 17, 1995

Marty was in a bad mood when I came home. I hate feeling so nervous around him. I feel emotionally abused.

Michael's transfer to Kentfield also had a substantial impact on my parents. My mother now had to drive from Scotts Valley to Marin County. The four freeway changes and the drive across the city of San Francisco were extraordinarily difficult for her. As in the past, my dad functioned as her navigator. My parents would spend several days at the Corte Madera Inn each week, dividing their time between Scotts Valley and Marin County and never really knowing how long they would be needed at either end. My mother expressed it well when she said, "Your father and I are the ones who can drop everything and be with Michael." They led their lives in limbo. It goes without saying that my mother gave up playing bridge entirely and she rarely participated in social activities of any kind during this period.

David and Joe drove from their home in San José to Marin County each weekend, occasionally staying overnight. It was a tremendous sacrifice for a pair of young men to spend their free time going to a hospital. Neither of them ever complained nor mentioned they would prefer to be anywhere else. Often Joe brought his basset hound, Casie, and she functioned as a therapy dog, nudging and kissing Michael and bringing a smile to his face. Joe and David would accompany Michael to therapy and push his wheelchair for walks in the neighborhood around the hospital.

Our staggered (and staggering!) visitation schedule with Michael prevented us from seeing each other very often. To solve this, we developed a communications system at the hospital. David suggested that we get a wipe off board where we could leave messages. We also designated a place to put packages or bags for each other. There were pens and paper available to write notes. And, of course, we called each other to report any news once the visit was completed.

December 27, 1995

> *I am concerned about everyone. My mom is overwrought. My dad is despondent and seems old. David smokes too much and is now out of a job. I worry Joe will get sick of all of us. Marty is tired and has lost too much weight and I am back on the precipice.*

8

Rate Your Hell

*T*he first few years after Michael's accident, I invented a mental game called "Rate Your Hell." To play, you think about whatever awful things are currently happening and compare them to other gut-wrenching things you've already been through. Although the stages of Michael's ordeal changed over time, things didn't necessarily get easier. Despite this, I usually imagined that I would prefer the present issues to past ones.

A new opportunity to play Rate Your Hell took place in March when the Kentfield treatment team announced at a team meeting that Michael probably had global aphasia, a speech therapy term meaning that would never be able to read, write or understand language again. It was a horrifying phrase to hear, but one I was familiar with. David had mentioned that it was a common outcome for people with Michael's level of injury.

At first I didn't get it. I asked, "Will he be able to learn some other system like sign language?" "No," she explained, "he won't be able to make sense of any type of language." Apparently the brain connections responsible for processing language were simply broken. I was devastated. Up to now, I thought that if we could somehow communicate with Michael we could create a survivable life. The global aphasia diagnosis washed away my hopes of having any meaningful interactions with him.

Dr. Doherty told me that there were some recovering stroke patients on Unit II who were aphasic. I studied the patients as I wandered up and down the halls of the unit, trying to figure out who had the condition. I imagined what it must be like to hear only garbled sounds coming out of someone's mouth. One afternoon I observed an interaction between a patient and a staff member on Unit II. The agitated patient was stretching and arching out of her wheelchair, pointing to the TV while making nonsense sounds. The staff person calmly responded with words which were obviously lost on the woman. Is this what it would be like with Michael? I couldn't even imagine. After watching this scene I thought to myself, If Michael has global aphasia, it's the all-time winner of Rate Your Hell.

Fortunately, this piece of hell didn't last long. About a month later, Michael was in a session with Dvora, his Kentfield speech therapist, when he saw the word "window" written on a piece of paper on her desk and pointed to the window in the room! Dvora called me immediately and I was thrilled and tremendously relieved by the news. Michael didn't have global aphasia. He understood language! Soon we discovered that, when asked, he could follow simple verbal directions, such as writing his name. He made no attempt to speak.

April 16, 1995

Michael seems more alert and the casting is definitely helping him sit better in the wheelchair. I still find it hard to believe that this accident happened and that Michael is so changed. I see him in my mind walking across the lawn. I wonder if I will have the strength and resolve to do everything possible for him.

May 2, 1995

Mother and Papa went to the hospital today and Michael had a terrific day. He blew out matches and a candle. He also blew three bubbles and identified five objects out of ten correctly. His nurses report he is following more and more commands. Wow!

May 9, 1995

Today I arrived at 8:45 A.M. and you were dressed and ready for p.t. with Elizabeth and W.W. I watched and took a few pictures. P.T. is hard work, but you're doing very well. When we were back in your room, we did some painting. Well, actually, you painted and I dealt with the ramification of your creativity like wiping up the

floor, washing your hands and arms up to the el-
bows and cleaning the paint cups! After that we
played a little with the Velcro ball. I went to your
speech session with Dvora. You wrote you name
and correctly identified a brush and a fork.

May 10, 1995

Today you scored 78 on the WNSSP! Wow!
Everyone is so jazzed.

Having the Western Neuro Sensory Stimulation
Profile score go up meant Michael was making cognitive progress. While we welcomed these latest improvements, they also brought him full-bore into the
agitated-confused behavior characteristic of Level 5
on the Rancho Los Amigos scale, the other important
measurement tool for patients recovering from a severe
brain injury. All of these patients must endure Level 5
in order to get to the next stage, just like every parent
must endure "the terrible twos." It was a very difficult
stage for Michael, for the hospital staff, and for us as a
family.

May 15, 1995

Michael has become an absolute terror! He is
very active and is often attempting to or succeed-
ing at pulling hair, pinching or biting someone.
Last week he bit two nurses. Today he pulled out
his gastrostomy tube and had to go back to the
hospital to have it replaced. Michael is at level 5

on the Rancho Scale which is characterized by inappropriate behavior. He may have brought "inappropriate behavior" to new heights! He takes the brakes off the wheelchair and rolls over to the nearest bulletin board where he takes everything off or to the nearest counter where he tosses items on the floor. He is getting some anti-anxiety medicine and it does help. It is a very difficult stage for us because he is obviously frustrated and tormented. It is a difficult stage for the hospital because he has to be closely watched. But, life demonstrates how everything is relative. Michael is the envy of three other families of young people (two 17-year-old girls and one 20-year-old girl) who are not making progress. All three are basically in the persistive vegetative state which is a dreadful thing to hear and contemplate. Whenever we think what we are going through is tough, we remember how any of these families would trade places with us.

During this phase Michael was extremely oral and everything went into his mouth –papers he pulled from the bulletin boards, plastic washbasins, hairbrushes, and my purse! He also did an excessive amount of drooling. With the help of the Unit 3 psychologist, Bill Daily, we came up with the idea of choosing something specific for Michael to put in his mouth. I made a trip to the San Rafael Toys-R-Us and bought 8 or 10 teething rings like you would give an infant. I remember the salesperson asked me, "Are you selecting something for your grandchild?" "No," I responded, as I played out in my mind what it would be like to explain that I was buying these for my 23-year-old son.

Bill Daily also had the clever idea of tying a teething ring to the wheelchair so one was always available. A string hung over the chair and when instructed to "get the chewy," Michael would slowly pull up on the string until he came to the teething ring, which he'd put in his mouth.

May 27, 1995 (written by David)

You are biting everything in sight and so we spent about half the time painting and the other half trying to keep you from biting the paintbrush, my clothes and the woman next to you at the table! We played catch with a Nerf ball, too, and you did very well, although at one point I turned around to find you had taken the big flip-top lid off one of the garbage cans and were just about to put it in your mouth.

May 29, 1995

Dr. Doherty told me that in 10 years she's only seen one person "stuck" in a very oral stage. She believes Michael will move out of this phase.

The drooling was a problem for Michael because it meant his clothes were always wet and he was often cold. After much thought, I decided to try buying a few inexpensive chef's aprons for him to wear. I pinned a folded towel inside the top bib of the apron to absorb most of the moisture, which kept his shirt dry. Michael wore these apron rigs at Kentfield for several months and the system turned out to be a good one.

After three months of serial casting on his legs, Michael was evaluated by an orthopedist, Dr. Michael Oechsel. At this point Michael's left leg was 20 degrees short of straight, his right leg 35. Oechsel felt surgery would help Michael. He proposed to lengthen the tendons at the knees and ankles. In order to uncurl the toes, the tendons would be severed. There was so much surgery involved that Dr. Oechsel said he would only do one leg at a time and allow about three weeks in between for Michael to recover. Each leg was to remain in a postoperative cast for six weeks.

I spoke to Dr. Doherty, the Kentfield Medical Director about the surgery before making my final decision. She said to me, "It will hinder Michael's cognitive progress if he can't sit appropriately and comfortably in a chair." One day at the SPCA I saw a friend of mine, Jan Nelson, who is paraplegic. I asked her, "What do you think of putting Michael through this very painful surgery just for the chance to walk?" She said without hesitation, "I would go through it just for the chance to stand, let alone walk!" These opinions helped me make the decision to move forward with the surgery.

June 28, 1995

David thinks we should ask Michael if he wants the surgery and not do it if he says, "no."

I don't think Michael is at the cognitive level to make such a decision. Wish David and I were more in sync about the medical decisions.

On July 28, Michael began to undergo the extensive surgery that was to take place on his left leg. Marty didn't go to the hospital with me, so I spent 6 hours alone in the surgery waiting room. When it was completed at about 7 o'clock, Dr. Oechsel came out to speak to me. "Just about everything we do we've done to Michael." He told me he cut himself on a scalpel during the operation and asked, "Has Michael been tested for HIV?" I said, "Yes, but please test him again if that will make you more comfortable."

Among the mumbo-jumbo of the insurance company's rules was one which required that Michael stay overnight at the hospital if a certain surgery suite was used. Because of this rule, he was slated to spend the night at Marin General Hospital and return to Kentfield the next morning. I didn't like this plan because the staff at Kentfield knew Michael where he was a total unknown at Marin General. Knowing just how to finesse Michael was so crucial to getting any kind of successful cooperation out of him; this was more than an idle concern.

Once Michael was out of the recovery suite, I walked down the hospital hall to the double room which had been assigned to him. There I faced a young male nurse who knew nothing about Michael. Soon another nurse arrived, a woman this time, and she asked me a series of questions. There was so much to tell her about Michael – he had such specific needs. I thought to myself, I can't possibly educate these people about Michael by answering a bunch of questions! I knew that without constant supervision he could easily fall out of bed, or yank out some of the various tubes and IV lines that inevitably accompanied these procedures. Marin General would not supply round-the-clock care because the insurance wouldn't pay for it, so Kentfield sent over one of their certified nursing assistants who arrived at around 10 P.M. I stayed for a little while until I was sure Michael was pain-free and could sleep, then I went back to the Corte Madera Inn to try and get some much-needed sleep myself.

I never asked anyone what the surgery had cost. We had met the deductible on Michael's insurance policy long ago and I assumed that Blue Cross would pay the balance. By now the company must have paid out hundreds of thousands of dollars, but surely less than the $5M cap which was advertised with the policy.

June 30, 1995

Michael didn't have a good day. His temperature went up to 102 degrees and he was pale. The doctor increased his pain medication and by afternoon his temperature was down to 101 degrees and he seemed calm. Oh how I hate the hell we have subjected Michael to.

The surgery on Michael's left leg was a breeze compared to what happened when the team tackled his right leg on September 29, 1995. After nearly six hours in the OR, Dr. Oechsel came out to tell Marty and me the operation was over and had gone well. It was about 11:00 P.M. The doctor told us we could go into the recovery room and see Michael. We walked through the swinging double doors to see Michael on a table, alone in the center of this huge, deserted, and dimly lit room – writhing in pain. He didn't make a sound but his face was terribly contorted and he kept lifting his right leg (in a thick cast from hip to toe) off the table. There were several large spots where blood had seeped through the cast. I tentatively asked the only nurse on duty, "Michael seems to be in considerable pain. Can he have more medication?"

At this late hour of the night, it seemed the entire hospital had been evacuated. The nurse told me, "I have to reach the doctor for authorization before I can give more pain medication." She picked up the phone to dial, then left a message on the recorder that answered.

An agonizing amount of time passed before the phone rang with the doctor's response. Yes, Michael could have more pain medication. An injection was added to one of his IV lines as I anxiously waited for a response, but the violent fits continued. The drug hadn't helped at all! Finally, Marty and the nurse figured out that the cast was too tight on the back of Michael's leg, causing at least part of his pain.

I was in a panic and my heart was racing. I felt angry that Michael hurt so much and no one was there who could fix it. Why hadn't the staff noticed his severe reaction earlier and done something about it? I kept pacing the room, each moment an hour. Seeing that I was absolutely unable to bear the situation, Marty said to me, "You go back out to the waiting room and I'll stay."

While I was gone, the nurse and a technician took a knife and cut away a small part of the cast. It seemed to bring almost immediate relief to Michael. Once he was calm, Marty came out to the waiting room to assure me that things were better and I could return to the recovery room. I argued against the overnight stay rule and this time Marin General agreed, allowing Michael to return to Kentfield immediately. He did seem to be in less pain, but the three days following this surgery proved to be very difficult.

October 17, 1995

The horrendous orthopedic surgery on Michael's right leg took place two weeks ago and it seems the worst is over. He was in terrific pain for about three days after it and I wasn't sure I was going to be able to stand it. He was on heavy-duty pain medication, including morphine and he ran a fever of over 102 degrees. I was totaled.

I've told a number of people I was very lucky the first surgery went so well. If Michael's right leg had been done first, I don't know if I would have had the courage to do the left. Maybe the doctor thought about this and knew exactly what he was doing in the scheduling. I am very glad we went forward with the surgeries because they made a tremendous difference in his ability to have a more normal life. Before the operations, Michael couldn't sit properly in a wheelchair; he was pulled downward in the chair by the flexures at his knees. He couldn't wear shoes because they did not fit his contorted feet, and the bend of his legs meant walking was out of the question.

Michael's cognitive progress slowly continued at Kentfield.

August 8, 1995

I see some improvements in Michael. He is mouthing the words, "Mom" "Michael" and "David." He is pretty consistent about shaking his head "yes" and "no." Today during speech Dvora was getting Michael to blow and form words. She said to Michael, "We're helping you speak. Do you want to speak to us?" Michael shook his head, "no" and I had to laugh. I also did some smelly things and started out with the onion. I asked Michael if he liked it and he shook his head "no." Then I showed him a paper with "onion" and "jasmine" written on it and asked him what he'd smelled and he pointed to the word onion! During speech with Ruth today she presented him with several lists and he had to scratch the thing out that didn't belong such as red, blue, whale, orange. Michael did three sets of these correctly. I think he knows more than we can determine due to the lack of a communication system. He is putting fewer things in his mouth.

August 29, 1995

Saturday when Marty and I were at Kentfield playing with the frog beanbags, Michael smiled spontaneously for the first time since the accident (more than a year ago). What a happy day. It was good to have Marty go with me to Kentfield. He drove up and I drove home.

Another wonderful thing happened in November which told me Michael still had a sense of humor.

November 11, 1995

Today I brought you a fabric turkey and I put it up on the wall next to your clock. Later in the day I asked you, "Where is the turkey?" and very quickly, you pointed to me! It was the funniest thing you have done since your accident. I loved it!

Michael was beginning the long process of learning how to eat again. As a first practice food, one of the speech therapists put a small amount of chocolate pudding in his mouth. It slid right out and onto a bib. Over and over again, the pudding went in and back out of

Michael's mouth while the speech therapist said, "Michael, move the food back in your mouth."

October 13, 1995

> *Right now you are eating with Cathy and being filmed for the insurance company review. You are eating a fruit shake and some vanilla pudding. It takes you 3 to 4 seconds to move the food back in your mouth and swallow. The average for a normal person is 1 second.*

The feeding tube remained connected to Michael's stomach because at this rate he wasn't getting enough calories by mouth. The process of learning to eat went on for several months, progressing from pudding to various kinds of pureed foods. The hospital was very careful about observing Michael's swallowing to ensure that food wasn't going into his lungs, which could cause aspiration pneumonia.

December 11, 1995

> *During this week when Dvora asked Michael what he wanted to eat he wrote, "solid." We all considered this a pretty sophisticated way to tell us he's sick of baby food!*

Michael was slowly improving, but would it be enough to satisfy the ever-present insurance company? Our case manager at Kentfield explained that he had to make "significant progress in a reasonable amount of time" in order to meet the insurance company standards. If he didn't do so, the company would stop paying for his treatment.

Blue Cross required that the Kentfield therapists produce regular videotapes of their sessions with Michael at two-week intervals. Based on what they saw, the company would approve Michael's stay for another two weeks. In between, there wasn't much time to relax. It seems incredible to me now that such a big decision would be made in two-week intervals. At the time, it made me feel as if a huge iron safe was always hanging over my head.

In talking about this issue at our Del Mar Caregivers support group meeting, I learned from the mother of another brain injury survivor that she had hired an attorney to help deal with her insurance company. In fact, several of the members of the group had experience with a particular personal injury attorney, a man in Santa Cruz named Robert Ludlow, Jr. whom they recommended. I decided to contact Bob right after the meeting to see if he would help me fight Blue Cross for the care Michael needed.

During my initial meeting with Bob, I explained Michael's continuing rehabilitation and told him I needed his help in getting the insurance company to pay. He agreed to work with me. I paid him a $500 retainer fee and signed some papers he referred to as engagement documents. "Would it be all right if I look into the details of the accident as well as working on the insurance?" he asked. "Sure," I said.

It was a number of months before I heard anything else from Bob. Eventually he called me to arrange a meeting in his Santa Cruz office. He said he had located and purchased the wrecked Ford Festiva in order to have it analyzed for failure. "I hired a safety engineer to look into the road conditions," he explained. "It appears the road shoulder didn't meet the minimum standards set up by the State of California. In addition, the Volvo was making an illegal left-hand turn into an illegal beach parking lot." Bob thought there was sufficient evidence of negligence to bring suit against Ford and the State of California.

I was absolutely shocked to find out the accident might not have been completely Michael's fault. It had never occurred to me to have a lawyer look into the details of the accident to determine all the facts. It was naïve to think the official police accident report was beyond question. Now I know it is always prudent to have an attorney examine a catastrophic case. The intensive investigation and review that an attorney can provide often results in financial recovery and medical benefits coverage, even if it originally appears that no recovery is possible. I learned that it is important to contact an attorney early as many legal issues are subject to a statue of limitations – an expiration date that, once passed, ends your chance to file a lawsuit.

Dr. Doherty wrote a letter about Michael's prognosis indicating he would never be able to hold a job, drive a car, or be able to stand trial. As a result, the

Santa Cruz District Attorney's office dropped the vehicular manslaughter charge against him.

September 6, 1995

> *Things have not been going well for Michael as he's been depressed and withdrawn. Yesterday in therapy he wrote, "I am crazy." We are all distraught that he feels this. So much about this just tears me apart emotionally. As time has gone by it hasn't really gotten easier, just different. I have terminal fatigue.*

October 30, 1995

> *Emotionally I feel totally out of control. I think I have to take a break from going to Kentfield. I am simply exhausted and I never seem to recover. I'm back on sleeping pills because I can't sleep though the night without them.*

I don't do anything well. At work I'm impatient and try to avoid new assignments and challenges. At home I don't make decent meals, I don't keep up the yard, I don't walk the dogs or play with them often. I don't keep up the house. I've lived my life attempting to avoid being "average" - doing things well - now I don't do anything at even the "average" level. I feel depressed and old and at a loss for what to do about anything.

The stress and sadness from Michael's accident took a huge physical toll on me. I felt dreadful and decided I needed to see my doctor, Nancy Greenstreet.

She and I agreed on a medical leave of absence from work for a couple of weeks. The time off was certainly helpful, but not enough to overcome my deep fatigue. The long period of sustained stress had given me a number of chronic physical complaints. The top of my shoulders hurt. My neck hurt. I had frequent indigestion. Strangely, my eyes hurt for days on end. At some point, my lack of energy and the various discomforts started to seem normal, as if dragging myself around was the usual thing to do. I would occasionally lock my door at work and lie down on the floor for 15 minutes just to take a break. At home I went to bed at 8:30, feeling like it was midnight.

Marty and I continued in our numb existence. I worked Monday through Thursday and went to Kentfield every Friday, mostly alone. Neither of us had the energy for anything fun; we both felt physically exhausted.

Marty and I had discussed on a few occasions what would happen when Michael was finally discharged from his long series of hospital stays. I knew we couldn't handle having him live with us, but I did want him to be able to visit. Our house is a split-level, probably the worst possible design for someone in a wheelchair. It did have the advantage of a very large family room on the lowest level. During one of these discussions with Marty I suggested, "Let's have an architect draw up plans to make the family room handicapped accessible." Surprisingly, he agreed.

The project called for turning the current bathroom into a wheelchair accessible one, and we would also have to get rid of the carpet downstairs. In September 1995, we hired architect Bill Fisher to redesign the room for Michael. Bill estimated the remodel costs at $12,000 to $15,000. Despite his initial agreement, Marty changed his mind, saying, "We don't have the money to do this." Michael had been receiving $600 a month in Social Security benefits and I had saved a year's worth. Certain we could afford it, I pleaded with him, "How can we not do this?" I desperately wanted Marty's agreement and consent (and I dreamed of his participation), but even if he didn't agree with my plans, knowing the house had to be made accessible for Michael, I forged on.

Michael's case manager at Kentfield started talking to me about his final discharge in the fall of 1995. She anticipated that Blue Cross would cease payments at the end of the year. I was terrorized at the thought of what was next for him. If he required nursing care at the time of his release, Michael would be discharged to a subacute facility. Although a subacute would tend to his medical needs, no therapies would be provided to help his communication or comprehension (speech therapy); to teach him to sit, stand, or walk (physical therapy); or even to provide the most basic of self-care (occupational therapy). I thought to myself, how can he get better without therapy?

When he no longer needed subacute care, the insurance would stop payments altogether. Michael would be discharged to a Medicaid bed in a SNF, pronounced "sniff." It stands for Skilled Nursing Facility, or what we commonly call a nursing home. I couldn't imagine Michael in a nursing home. I wouldn't let it happen. Every mention of the discharge plans gripped me with fear. I told myself, He can't be discharged! I don't know how to take care of him!

I was certainly glad I had pursued the serial casting and the orthopedic surgery. Both procedures had resulted in a longer stay at Kentfield. While he was there, he continued to receive speech therapy, PT, and OT, all of which helped him cognitively. In retrospect, these costly therapies had a life-changing impact on Michael. Without the "legs issue," I don't think Michael would have been able to stay at Kentfield for more than a few months.

These days, much of my time was consumed with working out ways to keep the insurance company paying for treatment. I tried to buy Michael some time between Kentfield and the nursing home. I needed to find out what other patients did after Kentfield so I asked Michael's case manager, who responded, "People with significant private money go to transitional living centers." She explained that these centers were not hospitals or long term care facilities but group homes where brain injured people stay for a short period of time to learn community reentry skills. I was somewhat familiar with the concept because San Jose Medical Center had its own large transitional skills training area. It featured 3-dimensional sets where clients could practice everyday activities, such as the front of a real bus which clients could learn to board. There was a grocery store check out stand where clients could practice shopping, and a restaurant section to experience reading a menu, ordering, and paying the bill – at least in theory. I had never actually seen anyone in this area. The case manager wasn't encouraging, either, quickly adding, "I've never seen Blue Cross pay for one of our patients to go to one."

I contacted Bob Ludlow and we went to work on a plan to get Michael into a transitional living center. Bob's approach was very low key and non-threatening. His message to Blue Cross again and again was, "It's probably prudent to go the extra mile with Michael, to provide more care and more support in order to avoid an accident or illness which would result in an even greater financial outlay for the company." Frankly, I think the insurance company paid attention because we had an attorney. By November 1995, it looked promising that Blue Cross might pay for transitional living and we began the hunt for the right place.

In the hope that Michael could finally be closer to home, my mother and I visited Learning Services in Gilroy, an hour and half southeast of our house. The center was on a large piece of property with a handful of single-story buildings. We met the director who gave us a tour. I thought, everything looks and smells clean, but I'm not sure how Michael will do with the shared bedroom situation. There was an on-site vocational program and some farm animals, which appealed to me. The staff was friendly and I found out Michael would get physical and speech therapy. The residents seemed pretty "out of it," but then Michael was too! Actually, I didn't want Michael to be in Gilroy or anywhere else. I wanted him back at home like he used to be.

Marty and I visited the second transitional living center in Dixon, California, which was 2 1/4 hours northeast of Scotts Valley. The program took place in a rural setting in a regular one-story home. The worst thing about the place was its name, Neurobehavioral Cognitive Services or NCS. I often thought, Whoever dreamed up the name should be shot! NCS seemed more intimate and home-like to me than Gilroy, and besides, they had a housedog. They accepted only six residents at a time, which I thought was a plus. As with the other facility, the staff here was nice, the place clean, the residents out of it – and Michael would get therapy. Ultimately we settled on NCS, even though Dixon was farther away. Once we made the decision, we had to wait to see if the center would accept Michael and if Blue Cross would actually pay the $25,000 per month that the program cost, and for how long?

I knew I had to figure out where people with brain injuries live permanently if they can't live at home. I found there are group homes which are not nursing homes and somewhere along the line a case manager gave me a list of places. They sounded good, with names like Golden Times and Country Gardens Care Home. I called several to find that they did not accept non-ambulatory clients. Others would not consider those who were below 7 on the Rancho Scale. At this point, Michael was still a Rancho 5 and likely to be in the wheelchair for some time, maybe forever. But that didn't matter. At $2,500 to $5,500 a month for long-term care, I had no hope of getting Michael into to a private residential group home anyway.

Continuing my search, I made an appointment with Lois Del Somes of the Del Mar Caregivers, the support group I had been attending. I had it mind to ask her, "Where are people like Michael expected to live?" I couldn't get it through my head that there was no place except a nursing home. I thought to myself again and again, Why spend hundreds of thousands of dollars to save people like Michael and then send them to nursing homes for the rest of their lives? I was still suffering under the misconception that all I needed was to find the right person who could give me a different answer.

Lois confirmed that there weren't any places. She looked me straight in the eye and said, "Jody, you will have to do it yourself." She continued, "Just think of it as renting a house, hiring attendants, and moving Michael in." I felt as if Lois had grabbed me and given me a big shake – just the shake I needed. I left her office knowing that I had to put aside the search for a place and instead commit myself to creating that place.

Joe Lambinas and Michael in 1994

From the left, David Bethune, Michael, Bill
Cramer, Jody, Marty Paterniti, Patty Cramer

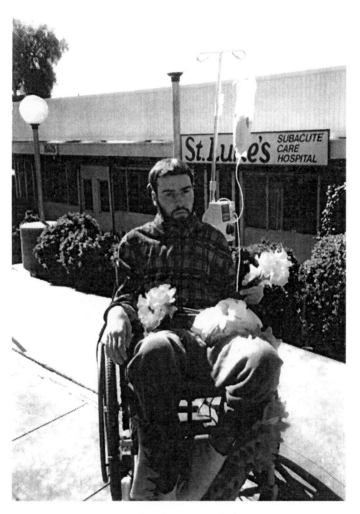

Michael at St. Luke's

At Kentfield

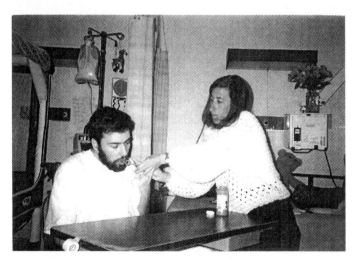

Working with Devora, the speech therapist

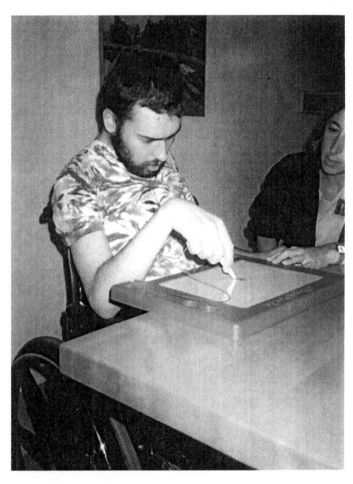

Learning to write again

I love
you
michael
want iz please!
Wan't
me to go
home

please

send

some
chocolate
fudge
I'm huge I

Dr. Deborah Doherty with Michael

An Optima bed

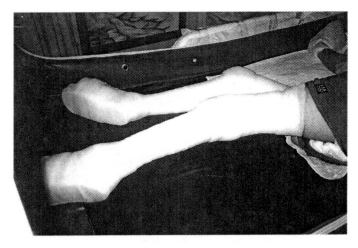

Michael's legs during serial casting

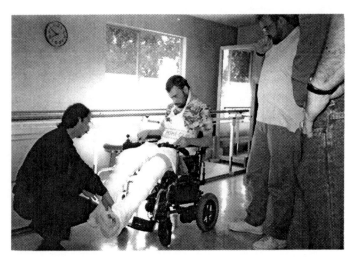

Physical therapy at Kentfield

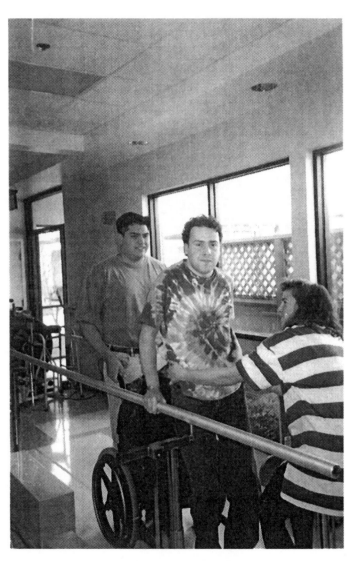

Learning to stand

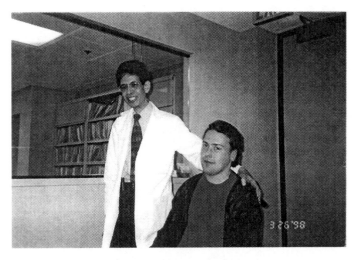

Michael visits his neurosurgeon,
Dr. Saadi in 1998

Michael with his brother David and
David's partner, Joe Rodriquez

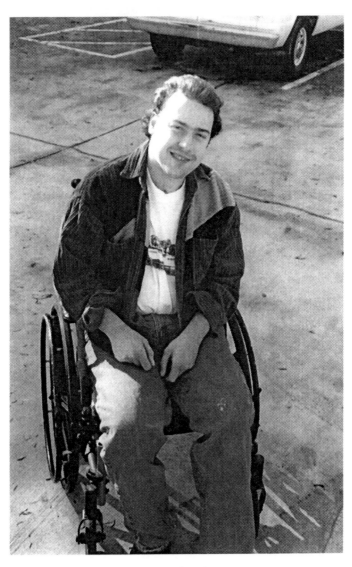

Michael today

9

Brave People

One day during the fall of 1995, Bob Ludlow called me and said, "I don't think Michael was the driver of the Ford." Several things pointed to Joe Lambinas as the driver. First, the man who pulled the two young men out of the car had identified Michael as the passenger. The man in the driver's seat was dead. Secondly, although the steering wheel was missing from the Festiva when Bob bought it, a photo of the wheel revealed indentations that looked like tooth marks. Lambinas had lost both front teeth in the accident. In addition, a medical engineer told Ludlow that Michael's injuries were consistent with his having been the passenger.

I was both relieved and upset to receive this information. I kept thinking, We have lived for more than a year believing that Michael was responsible for someone else's death! I was also upset because the incorrect police report had led to comments about Michael's reckless driving appearing in the local newspaper. The same error also triggered an investigation by the District Attorney and the resulting vehicular manslaughter charge, which was eventually dropped.

Bob told me he wanted to bring in a San Francisco attorney named Michael Moore, a product liability specialist. Ludlow explained, "If Michael was the passenger, he had no responsibility for negligence and could therefore possibly receive a substantially higher settlement." I was very glad that I'd engaged Bob and that he investigated the accident so thoroughly, but I had neither the energy nor the time to closely follow the case developments. In the early stages of a trauma, the family is too stressed-out to carefully weigh the legal implications of the accident. This makes it all the more important to hire a good attorney early on.

My reputation as the person with a calming effect on Michael had followed me to Kentfield and soon I was trying to work my magic in some very new situations. On April 28, 1995, Michael was admitted to Marin General Hospital for a feeding tube replacement. I was waiting with him for the OR nurses who would take the gurney into the operating room when I learned that the anesthesiologist scheduled to supervise the general anesthesia was busy with another surgery. Michael's gastroenterologist, Dr. Bloom, asked me, "Would you consent to having Michael heavily sedated instead of completely anesthetized?" He assured me Michael wouldn't feel any pain. When I agreed, he offered, "It would be terrific if you would come into the surgery suite with us and calm Michael." For most of my life, I had been very queasy about needles and, medical procedures and wounds, but I learned I could rise to the occasion when it came to Michael. I donned the surgical gown and gloves there in Michael's room and followed a nurse into the surgery suite.

I stood right next to the anesthesiologist at Michael's head. I watched while the doctor started the IV and in a very few minutes Michael was asleep. Dr. Bloom then put an endoscope tube through his mouth down to his stomach. There was a camera at the end of the tube and I could see inside Michael's stomach in color on a TV monitor. It was fascinating. The procedure took about 15 minutes and about 10 minutes after that Michael was awake. While he was asleep, I did a beard trim. A little surgery, a little barbering.

I was gaining confidence about facing medical procedures and feeling more and more comfortable in my role as the designated brain. Denise Young, Michael's case manager at Kentfield, agreed to be available to meet with my mother when she had concerns. Mother felt better having a specific contact and this created less chaos than going to several staff members with a question.

Meanwhile, I continued the philosophy of not sweating the small stuff. I learned that if I wanted something to change, I needed to talk to Dr. Doherty. If a situation were truly urgent, I would leave a message with her secretary or ask that she be paged. If it were not urgent, I would compile a list and make an appointment to see her. I was sure to arrive on time and take notes so that I could pass on information accurately to the rest of the family.

One of the issues that I thought important enough to go to the doctor about was the fact that Michael's room was consistently too cold. Another issue came up when Michael was in a very noisy active room, with the result that he seemed over stimulated. I also considered it a serious issue when I found the hospital in a state of disarray one weekend. The hospital floors weren't clean; tables in the family gathering room were covered with trays of dirty dishes and trashcans hadn't been emptied. I found out later that there had been some changes in the housekeeping staff.

One of the most serious issues concerned a staff member who didn't seem to be caring for Michael appropriately. My family and I noted a couple of disturbing things, such as the fact that this person didn't change Michael promptly when he had a bowel movement. I had my facts together when I wrote a very polite letter to the hospital administrator, documenting our concerns and asking that the person not be assigned to Michael again. The administrator promptly responded, granting our request.

Nine months is a long time to be in any hospital. It's to be expected that problems will occur. For the most part, Kentfield was a terrific, professional place and I am very grateful that Michael was able to be there.

In the fall of 1995, during one of our regular meetings, Dr. Doherty asked me, "Would you be willing to give Michael a drug called bromokriptine which might help him speak?" The drug was actually developed to stop lactation in nursing mothers. In some cases, it seemed to help brain injured patients begin speaking again and had been used somewhat experimentally for that purpose.

Doherty explained, "Science doesn't know exactly what the drug does in the brain, but some of my patients started talking after they had reached the therapeutic dose." She warned me that some patients had stopped talking once they went off of the drug. I was very enthusiastic to try anything that might help Michael to speak and I urged her to go ahead with the bromokripitine. During the week that Michael reached the therapeutic dose, he spoke out loud for the first time in 16 months!

December 14, 1995

> *Michael spoke today! He said, "Fuck you" to his physical therapist, Christina. She was overjoyed and hugged and praised him, telling him, "Say it again! Say it again!"*

I was not at all surprised by Michael's first words. I had been around other patients at Kentfield when they first spoke and these seemed to be the most popular choice. Dr. Doherty explained, "Often people must be driven by an extreme emotion before they speak and anger is usually it." Michael didn't talk again until the first week in January. That's when I heard his voice on the phone.

January 10, 1996

> *When I said "Hi" he said "Hi" back to me. I could hardly believe it so I asked him to say it*

again and he did! Then he said, very clearly, I love you! I really did not expect Michael to speak again. I had just sealed myself not to be disappointed if it didn't happen. I knew we would find a way to communicate. Bless his heart, Michael is the bravest person I've ever known. He is an absolute inspiration.

I continued to attend meetings of the Del Mar Caregivers to Brain Injured Adults group where I met and got to know Crystal Dunniway. In many ways, we were an odd couple. Crystal is a devoutly religious person who attends a Christian Orthodox church in the small mountain town of Felton, California. Despite my background, I'm basically a non-religious person. Crystal is conservative and, although I never asked her, I'll bet she's a Republican. I'm a liberal Democrat, a vegetarian, an animal rights activist and, very openly, the mother of two gay sons.

At times I felt like my family shocked Crystal, although she never said so. The things we had in common, however, outweighed our differences. We seemed to be soul mates from the very beginning, since our kids were about the same age, had both grown up in Santa Cruz, and had similar injuries. We naturally fell into the pattern of supporting each other. Crystal wrote this passage about her daughter, Michelle.

Michelle Dunniway was born in Saigon, Vietnam on October 29, 1974. Not much is known about her first six months, except that her biological mother was in her late forties and had five other children. She claimed she could not afford to feed another child and she signed Michelle over to the Friends of Children of Viet Nam (FCVN), so that she could be brought to the United States for adoption. Michelle escaped on one of the last planes to leave Viet Nam when it fell in the spring of 1975. FCVN brought her to their Denver headquarters because she had not yet been assigned to a family. We received a call on May 3 notifying us that a young infant girl was available for adoption and three days later we picked her up at the San Francisco Airport.

Michelle was a healthy, active child who was very verbal and excelled at almost anything she undertook. She attended Boulder Creek Elementary School, San Lorenzo Junior High and San Lorenzo Valley High School. She was an outstanding student and was involved in basketball, tennis and track.

After graduation from high school in 1993, Michelle enrolled at the University of California, Santa Barbara. The summer after her freshman year she came home and took a temporary job as a bookkeeper for Santa Cruz Auto Body. The job ended a couple of weeks before school started.

During spring finals a close friend of Michelle's was killed in a bike accident and she came home to attend the funeral taking an incomplete in two classes for missing the finals. The tuition rose sharply that fall and she did not have quite enough money to cover her sophomore year. At the very last minute she decided to wait until winter quarter to return to school. She planned to stay at home and work.

Around the middle of November she drove to Santa Barbara to attend a wedding and on her way back to Boulder Creek she was hit head on by a semi truck while driving through the Salinas area. She suffered a closed head injury and sustained serious brain stem damage. She remained in a hard coma for about two months. There was a 10-inch laceration on the left side of her head, a broken upper left arm, a broken pelvis, her right kneecap was shattered and she had multiple abrasions, bruises and cuts. One tooth was knocked out. After a few days a rod was put in her arm and the kneecap was reconstructed. A gastrostomy tube was inserted in her stomach through the wall of her abdomen and a trach was put in her throat.

Michelle had been covered under her father's medical insurance until October 31, 1994, two weeks prior to the accident. The insurance company had discontinued coverage because she was not a full-time student on her October 29 birthday. After the accident we were able to enroll her in continuation coverage because the sixty-day grace period following the termination of the insurance was still in effect.

About three weeks after the accident Michelle was moved from the ICU at Salinas Valley Memorial Hospital to a regular room at Dominican Hospital in Santa Cruz. At that point her eyes were slightly open but she was not responding to anything. A week later she was placed in the subacute rehabilitation unit at Pacific Coast Manor. In January she was admitted to Dominican with pneumonia and a collapsed lung. In late February she again had pneumonia and was re-admitted to Dominican.

Michelle left Pacific Coast Manor on March 15, 1995 and was admitted to Kentfield Rehabilitation Hospital in Marin County for eight weeks of drug trials as part of a coma stimulation program. She ended up staying an additional three weeks but showed very little progress. Her eyes were now wide open but she could not track movement. She seemed more and more alert but was virtually unresponsive. There was a subtle "total body response" when friends came to visit which lead us to believe she was recognizing them.

When her time was up I began searching for a nursing home because Pacific Coast did not have any openings. After contacting fifty-seven nursing homes, Winchester Convalescent Hospital in San Jose finally agreed to take her.

The insurance did not pay for "custodial care" so MediCal began picking up the bill for room and board. **Most nursing homes do not want to take young, catastrophically injured people who are on Medi-Cal and have a gastrostomy tube because it isn't cost effective for them.** *Michelle struggled along for thirteen months in the nursing home, spending most of her day in bed. She was put in her wheelchair about four hours a day and placed in the hallway where she watched elderly people wander back and forth. The doctor at the nursing home was not attentive to her needs and she was simply "warehoused" with the elderly. Toward the end of her stay there she developed a blood infection and ended up in Valley Medical Center for a couple of weeks.*

In March 1996 Michael's father (when the kids were growing up, I called him "Big David") came to visit from Oklahoma. He and Marty and I had discussed where Michael would go after rehabilitation. I had a very negative feeling about nursing homes, so I thought we all should experience one first hand. We went to visit Michelle at the Winchester Convalescent Hospital with the idea to use it as a research trip. As soon as we arrived, I went to the front desk and asked, "How many residents do you have and what is their age range?" I found out that the average age among the 140 patients was in the 70's. Michelle, at 20, was by far the youngest patient and the only one who wasn't a senior citizen.

We were directed down the labyrinth of halls toward her room. Along the way, we encountered a number of elderly people sitting in wheelchairs. The hallways were littered with medicine cabinets, dirty linen and dish carts, walkers, and the occasional staff member. We found Michelle in a room with three beds, sitting in her wheelchair, head down. Her roommates were elderly women, both of whom had dementia. They screamed constantly and said nonsensical things to no one. I thought, There is absolutely nothing normal here – nothing that a young woman can relate to. Actually, nothing that I can relate to! I felt so uncomfortable in the room that I asked Marty to help me push Michelle's chair out onto a patio where we spent about an hour with her. After this visit I felt totally committed to "springing" Michelle from this place, and to preventing Michael from ever going anywhere like it.

March 18, 1996

Sunday afternoon, Marty and I met David at the Winchester Nursing Home where Michelle Dunniway is a resident. What a horrendous, depressing place. We spent about 1 ½ hours with Michelle and left feeling totally sure that no nursing home will do for Michael.

10

Transitional Living

*I*n November, the case manager at Kentfield notified me that Blue Cross would pay for the transitional living program at Neurobehavioral Cognitive Services (NCS). On December 19th, Michael would be admitted to their facility in Dixon, California. I felt elated, knowing this was a victory over the insurance company.

On that Tuesday morning, Marty and I made the drive to Marin County to accompany Michael during the transfer. When we arrived at Kentfield we were told that he had a temperature and couldn't be released. After spending some time with Michael, we left for home, only to discover that the Golden Gate Bridge was backed up for hours. I slouched down in the passenger seat and allowed a terrible mood to possess me completely. I thought about how I hated my life, this car, the other cars, Marty, my aches, my pains, and the "accident card" I had been dealt.

We were back at Kentfield on December 21st for Transfer, Round 2. Leaving Kentfield after so much time was an emotional moment for us and for the members of Michael's team,. The staff made a very special t-shirt, signed by many of them and quoting a line from Shel Silverstein, Michael's favorite poet. At the departure get-together, I saw many smiles, hugs, and tears. I felt as if we were leaving home. Michael, on the other hand, seemed anxious to get out of Kentfield and excited about leaving. I packed our numerous supplies into cardboard boxes and loaded them in my pickup truck which Marty would drive for the hour and half trip to Dixon.

I rode in the ambulance with Michael. His wheelchair had to be strapped in the back, so I sat in the front passenger seat with my back to him. At some point I felt like I wanted to be closer to Michael, so I crawled out of my seat and went to sit on the floor beside him. I was there about fifteen minutes when Michael motioned for me to go back to my seat! I was impressed that he was thinking about my comfort and safety and wanted me back in a regular seat, and that he had figured out how to communicate nonverbally.

The moving day was very difficult. On top of meeting the new staff, we had brought too much stuff and now we had to deal with all of it. When we pulled into the NCS parking lot with out truckload of "necessary items," the co-director of the program, Carrie Jolander, came out and said very diplomatically, "There isn't room for all of these things you have brought. Would you please pick out some to bring in and take the rest home?" Feeling a little resentful about this, I proceeded to sort the items into "go" and "stay" piles.

NCS was, by design, very different from other facilities where Michael had been. Although there was a nurse on staff, the clients (who were no longer referred to as patients) were medically stable. At the time Michael joined the NCS family, there were four other neurologically impaired adult men living in the house and a day client who went home at night. There were four bedrooms and a few clients shared rooms. Some clients required continual supervision twenty-four hours a day by an NCS employee. The attendants rotated clients every hour or so. Michael was one of the clients assigned to a 24/7 attendant rotation.

The NCS facility was a typical ranch-style home in a very rural area of California's central valley. There were no other houses nearby, which I assumed helped to eliminate the issue of client escape. The layout was like any other suburban house. The living room had a TV, VCR, a computer and games. The bedrooms were furnished with beds and dressers from Goodwill. The place had a large kitchen, fully equipped, and I later learned that Louise, the NCS cook, prepared meals that both looked and smelled terrific. Clients ate at a couple of big tables in the family room. During the day, they spent their time going on outings, discussing current events, planning meals, playing games, and doing craft activities. The NCS staff consisted of a physical therapist, an occupational therapist, and a speech pathologist, so all clients had access to these therapies. To add to the mix, NCS had a housedog, a sweet black lab named Ezra.

Michael's two-person room was on the back of the house with a view of open farmlands from the window. His artwork went up on the walls along with some lists I had made of people he particularly liked, mostly artists and musicians. Since Michael had only recently graduated from the net-enclosed Optima bed at Kentfield, the NCS staff thought it would be best if we put side rails on his bed for the time being. I agreed.

2-17-96

> *NCS told me yesterday the licensing agency wouldn't let them have a bed with rails, which Michael has. So now his bed is on the floor. So many things about life feel absolutely absurd.*

I never achieved a feeling of comfort at NCS. I think it had to do with the fact that few families visited as often as we did and the staff didn't quite know what to do with me. I didn't know what to do with them either. With the round-the-clock supervision they provided, I always felt as if I were intruding. One major problem for me was that there was very little storage where I could put things, so I left a lot of things in the car. Sometimes I would bring in a bag from the car and inadvertently leave it in the living room. Soon, an attendant would bring it to me and I would know I had done the wrong thing. After several months at NCS, I was assigned a shelf in a locked closet, which meant I had to ask an attendant each time I wanted access. Being exhausted and drained, these small issues seemed immense.

I had some very difficult moments over one thing which now seems really silly. Whenever I visited, it seemed every staff person I encountered would ask, "How long are you going to stay?" and "Is someone else coming with you?" Intellectually, I knew they were just making conversation and trying to be nice, but in my burned-out state, I often thought that they were probing to see how long they would have to put up with me. Finally, I said something to the director about this and she assured me nothing could be further from the truth. By the time our family got to NCS we were all shell-shocked and weary -- far from normal and, without a doubt, a demanding and difficult crew.

1-1-96

I spent about two hours with Mom and Papa today. They are having a hard time with Michael's transition to Dixon as it is quite different from Kentfield.

We held the Second Hospital Christmas at NCS. Hoping to avoid another round of the dreadful food from the First Hospital Christmas, this year I decided to precook a turkey with dressing, gravy, mashed potatoes, and pumpkin pie. I would like to say that the family gathered around the NCS microwave to share our Christmas Eve dinner, but since it took about 5 or 6 minutes to heat each plate we basically wound up eating separately. A highlight of the evening was the frightening "gravy-like substance" that had been transported in a plastic container from Scotts Valley. After dinner we opened some presents, and this time Michael could actually open his own things.

We had completely taken over the NCS living room because that was where the Christmas tree had been put up, but apparently we were too loud. Around 8:00 P.M., a staff member asked us if we could "wrap it up" as another client was scheduled to watch a movie there. Another holiday faux pas was brought to my attention when I carried in an unopened case of imported beer for David and Joe. A staff person informed me that no alcohol was permitted on the premises. I think I must have forgotten to ask about the house "Do's and Don'ts!"

12-25-95

Last night Mother and Papa stayed at the NCS guesthouse while David, Joe, Marty and I stayed at the Best Western. Christmas Day we stayed with Michael until about 2:30 then drove home. When we got home I thought, Well, we're alive.

During our Christmas visit, my father wrote in Michael's hospital logbook for the very first time.

12-14-95 (written by Bill)

Christmas and our first visit to your new place. If you are good we will open some Christmas presents tonight - hope we can all wait. This is my first note in your daybook. I could never write in it before. Remember Christmas Eve day we always went to Carmel, ate in that hotel dining room, bought some presents then back to Scotts Valley to open all the presents. You are much improved and a great joy to all the family. Love, Papa

By the time Michael entered NCS his weight was down to 119 pounds. He had weighed 190 at the time of the accident. Sometime in January the staff told us he would have to begin to gain weight or he couldn't stay at NCS and would have to be hospitalized again. The feeding tube was no longer an option as Michael had pulled it out on December 31st and the hole quickly closed up.

We certainly didn't want him back in the hospital, so my mother and I went to work on a high-calorie diet for Michael. We made potato soup with cream and butter. We made pudding with half-and-half and scalloped potatoes with cream and potato salad with tons of mayonnaise. In tasting these treats I rediscovered the joy of fat. It tastes so good!

You might expect that if a person hasn't been able to eat for a long time he might be enthusiastic at the thought of eating again. But in my limited experience I never saw anyone who was thrilled about learning to eat. People had to be urged and cajoled into eating, sometimes even threatened with a hospital stay if they didn't start to eat. Other clients were told they would have to eat a certain amount in order to gain a special privilege. One factor, I think, is the fact that initially all the food is pureed, basically baby food and pretty unappealing. It took about four months from the time food was first introduced into Michael's mouth before he was able to eat without any encouragement. During this time, many people put forth a great effort to find the things Michael might like to eat and to work with him and encourage him to eat them.

1-3-96

Spoke with Dixon today. Michael has been eating 2 out of 3 meals. Dixon bought a scale that will weight Michael in the wheelchair. They've found a high calorie strawberry drink he likes. The staff tells me Michael is not sleeping well. I suggested having Ezra, the house hound, sleep in his room.

————————

My routine for NCS was to drive there on the third Friday of each month to spend the night and drive home on Saturday afternoon. It was a lot like the Kentfield visits, except the trip took about 30 minutes longer each way. Marty's attendance was definitely a rarity and I never counted on it.

1-4-96

I just returned from Dixon. This is the first time I've gone by myself and it was hard, but it's always hard regardless. Michael was bright and cheerful. I crammed as much as I could into the visit. We played with Play-Doh, painted both days, went outside and tossed the ball for Ezra. I brought a Michael Jackson video and Michael moved his head to the rhythm. He can repeat most of the words and I encouraged him to sing. We calculated our ages and Michael correctly subtracted 1996 from 1972 to arrive at his age of 24 and 1996 from 1945 to come up with my age of 51. Numerous times Michael told me he wants "to go home to 8 Suzanne Lane, Scotts Valley, California zip code 95066". Each time I replied we are in the process of remodeling the house so he can visit.

When several members of the family were at NCS together we would play board games or art lotto games with Michael. If he were in the mood, we could keep him involved for about thirty minutes. This was significant for him and a great improvement over the attention span he had shown up to now. I would also take a number of photo albums with me, using them to talk at length about family members or trips we had taken.

NCS offered what they referred to as "a guesthouse" and the staff told me our family could stay there. When I first heard about the guesthouse, I assumed it was an empty house in which families could stay. This was certainly welcome news as I had spent about $3,000 on motels already. The house was actually the home of the director's mother. She had two bedrooms, which were available for client families, and I began my visits to

Dixon by staying there. The lady of the house was a warm and charming woman who made me feel welcome, but I found it hard to relax in someone else's home.

During one visit, my mother and I went to sleep on the twin beds in the guestroom, but Mom's snoring was keeping me awake. I got up and went out to sleep on the living room sofa. There, I hit a glass knickknack on a nearby table and broke it. I felt awkward at NCS and awkward at the guesthouse. I seemed to be one big bumble and I kept thinking, I wish I could just get it together and behave like the competent adult I used to be.

After staying about four or five times at the guesthouse, I decided I had to find a suitable motel. The search proved more difficult than expected. The Corte Madera Inn had been so comfortable and easy to get to. Now I was outside Vacaville, the nearest large city, facing a huge strip of freeway lined with motels on each side. I tried a different one with each trip but all suffered from some inadequacy. One was cold and didn't have enough blankets. One was too noisy and one was too quiet, isolated and creepy. In the six months Michael spent at NCS, I never once felt settled about the place I spent the night. This fact, coupled with my loneliness, greatly added to the stress of my visits, but I felt a tremendous burden to carry on despite the travel, the time at NCS, and the lonely nights without my partner. For my parents, of course, NCS meant even more freeway driving

2-11-96

Mother drove herself and Papa to Dixon Friday and home Saturday. I had written out directions and she made it without a hitch. She is concerned Michael can't lie down comfortably and that is contributing to his lack of sleep. She did say he looks good and smiles often.

The plans had been drawn and approved for the remodel of our Scotts Valley house and a contractor had been selected. By the end of February we were waiting for his schedule to make it possible for him to begin.

2-20-96

Today was grim. I have the sinking feeling again I'm about to go out of control. Michael is becoming more and more insistent he wants to come home and it is breaking my heart that I can't simply make it happen. He says he wants to come home to Scotts Valley. I never knew this house or this town meant so much to him.

2-25-96

Friday and Saturday Marty and I went to Dixon. Michael has gained 24 pounds since arriving there and is up to 143. He looks really good! When we arrived he was sitting at the table eating with the other clients. It looked like such a normal scene. He's now on a regular diet without any restrictions.

Michael's cognitive progress continued at NCS. He was making a significant effort to talk and to be understood although his speech was slurred.

1-15-96

Michael said my full name was Jody Cramer and also said his birthday was March 15, 1972. We made some lists and Michael correctly spelled Van Gogh and corrected me when I wrote Matisse with only one s. His spelling is pretty impressive.

Following this visit, I bought Michael books about several of his favorite artists and mailed them to him one book at a time. NCS was also working with Michael on improving his mobility and on standing and walking.

2-25-96

Michael's movements appear almost "normal." Friday Leslie and Cathy had him practice walking. Michael put an arm around each therapist, rose from the chair and with great difficulty "walked" about 10 feet, all the time making the most mournful sounds.

Once Michael had found his voice, he used it to protest anything he didn't like. He would begin an "outburst" by screaming, "No!" He voice was so loud and deep that its sudden appearance was often quite shocking. The initial "no" would be followed by screaming that could be heard all over the house. Showering was always accompanied by screaming.

When it came to showering, Michael was absolutely defiant. It is an interesting phenomenon, the number of head-injured people who don't bathe, and a significant issue for those of us who are around them! Some of the theories I've heard include the notion that head-injury survivors usually have memory impairment and may not remember when they last bathed. One mother believed her son's tactile perceptions had been changed by his brain stem damage and he no longer liked the feel of water on his body. In fact, he didn't like to be touched at all. My observations with Michael lead me to believe he doesn't remember the last time he bathed. I do, and it was an awful lot of work!

Getting his clothes on and off is always a struggle since Michael can't stand on his own. At NCS, he developed the technique of putting on and taking off his pants on the bed. Lying on his back, he would lift his legs in the air and roll while working the pants up or down. After getting his clothes off, he had to transfer into a shower chair or onto a shower bench before washing and rinsing. I think most people really enjoy the feeling of warm water, but Michael does not. Next we dry off before transferring back to the regular wheelchair and then back to the bed to reverse the dressing routine.

Most of the clients at NCS have behavioral issues. Indeed, that is largely why they are there. The behavioral ramifications of head injury (and other neurological impairments) vary, but there are some behaviors which are very much to be expected.

Short-Term Memory Loss

People with even mild head injuries often experience changes in their ability to remember recent information. With more severe injuries comes increased short-term memory loss. Many survivors don't remember the little details of life that the rest of us take for granted, like what they had for lunch, what they did yesterday afternoon, or what movie they saw last night. People with severe short-term memory loss are forced to live completely in the moment. They experience chronic learning disabilities and require far more exposures to a fact or concept than others before they can integrate new information. Sometimes a brain injured person might literally need to be told something 50 times before he can remember it.

Inhibition

Head-injury frequently results in impaired inhibitions. The result is that survivors do things they would never have done before. At the Del Mar Caregivers support meeting, one survivor's wife told about the time she and her husband were walking on a very public beach when he suddenly stopped, unzipped his pants, and urinated. Neurologically impaired people may use excessive profanity, behave intrusively, or make inappropriate comments and sexual advances to strangers. They may create public, vocal outbursts or masturbate in front of others due to the loss of inhibiting factors in the brain.

Michael is in a wheelchair, so people are visually cued that he is disabled. But in ambulatory people with neurological impairment, the disability is usually invisible. Lack of inhibitors can lead to decreased anger control, possibly resulting in public aggression, police involvement, or arrest. From the research I did, I discovered that many brain-injured people end up homeless or in the penal system.

Attention Loss

Survivors are often impaired in their ability to focus and pay attention. They may complain of boredom, but they can't stay with an activity for very long. The loss of attention span makes it even more difficult for the brain injured person to re-learn their daily life skills.

Michael experienced *all* of these residual issues from his severe closed head injury. The professional staff at NCS was charged with evaluating Michael and designing a custom program which would help him modify his problematic behaviors and encourage his cognitive development.

When Michael had been at NCS for two weeks, the staff produced an initial report. It indicated that Michael could comprehend short phrases and was able to initiate activities in his immediate environment, such as drawing or painting, playing a familiar video, and interacting with the dog. He was unable to sustain attention for more than 5 to 10 minutes in any of these activities. Michael's attempts to write were evidence of poor mechanical skills, do to a lack of fine motor control. His letters were very large and often illegible and written on irregular lines at strange angles to the page. He could read haltingly at a basic word and phrase level.

The report noted that Michael was highly distractible and exhibited perseveration, a state in which he is "stuck" thinking about or talking about something over and over again. He also exhibited perseverative physical behaviors, such as insisting on repeatedly brushing his teeth or wheeling incessantly from room to room. Michael was also sometimes physically abusive -- biting, grabbing, pulling hair, and attempting to strike attendants. He threw objects, yelled, and swore. The staff at NCS thought much of Michael's aggression was the result of frustration, especially when people failed to provide an immediate response to his every want or need. He demonstrated significant loss of inhibition. At the time of admission, Michael was incontinent of both bowel and bladder. He did not initiate requests to be changed or give any sign that he needed to use the toilet.

I had many chances to observe the NCS strategy of praising and encouraging Michael when he did something correctly. The staff was very patient, attentive, and supportive. In order to increase Michael's attention span, he was allowed to choose an activity and then required to stay with it for a minimum of 10 or

15 minutes. The attendant would ask Michael, "What would you like to do for the next 15 minutes?" Once he chose an activity, the attendant set a timer while saying, "Okay, you'll need to stay with this for 15 minutes." If Michael wanted to leave the area where the activity was taking place, he was not allowed to do so. If he tried to move his wheelchair, the attendant physically stopped him. If Michael erupted into an outburst, the staff person would "wrap" him by standing behind the chair and wrapping his or her arms around Michael's arms and chest, preventing him from striking someone or throwing something. Michael hated being wrapped, but in time he got the message and the outbursts began to decrease.

———————

Michael had his 24th birthday at NCS and his father, David M. Bethune, arrived from Oklahoma for the occasion.

3-18-96

Michael opened his cards and presents, ate the dessert and seemed to have a very good time. At 3:00 PM we went to a local mall where Michael picked out his first pair of shoes (boots!) since his accident (he was prevented from wearing shoes for months after the surgeries because he had significant pressure sores on both heels from the casts). It was sure the same old Michael in that he had definite ideas about the color and style. He had his Dad and David and me really hopping around the shoe store to find something he liked. After that we went to the Jockey store to get Michael some underwear as he's wearing them now in the daytime. It was a good day.

4-3-96 [written by the program clinical manager]

"Michael's progress to date has been remarkable, especially considering he is almost 20 months post injury."

Despite his progress, we had no guarantee that Blue Cross was going to continue to pay for NCS. I wanted him to stay there because I hadn't yet resolved the issue of Michael's permanent residence. I had, however, begun in earnest to meet with some people about setting up a house for Michael.

3-1-96

Bob Ludlow is interested in coming to the meeting at Steve Bennet's. I really like Bob. He's intelligent, a dynamo and absolutely overflowing with ideas. He's working on helping us secure some money in the near future from State Farm which we might be able to use to set up a house.

3-9-96

Last Thursday Crystal Dunniway and I had lunch with Steve and Leslie Bennet. Their daugh-

ter, Leslie, has her own home with attendants. She's a brain injured paraplegic in a wheelchair. Steve gave us a copy of his budget for Leslie and I used it to put together a preliminary budget for our private housing project. We went to visit Leslie and tour her house. She's very high functioning, but her father says it took a long time.

My personal relationship with Marty continued at a tentative standoff.

3-4-96

Marty's been extremely tired. He's thin and really unhappy about his work. I worry about him. Yesterday I went to the office and helped him for about an hour. Today I arranged for him to have a massage. What he needs is more peace and quiet, better meals, less stress, more attention... all things I am totally incapable of providing in my current state.

3-10-96

I am feeling depressed about my relationship with Marty. I don't want to be the cause of his pain. Lately I've been thinking I should find a way to move out, but that is a daunting undertaking given what else is on my plate. Wish he weren't so terribly unhappy. I never wanted to be the contributor to his unhappiness.

Our contractor notified me that he could begin working on the remodel on April 16. I should have thought about the fact that this was the day after income tax season ends -- the first day off for Marty in many months and one when he especially needed peace and quiet. I don't know why I didn't think about it. I don't know why I didn't ask the contractor to start a week later, and I don't know why I didn't find out that the first thing he would do was destroy a wall in our home. It was an inauspicious beginning to a project for which Marty already had little enthusiasm.

4-18-96

Unfortunately on April 16 our contractor and company began the remodel of the downstairs. For two solid days the sound and vibration of a jackhammer used to break up a portion of the concrete slab dominated the house. Huge clouds of cement dust blanketed the entire house and contents in a thick, white film. The contractor had failed to mention to us that this might happen so we didn't have a chance to cover anything. Since Marty is already significantly exhausted this couldn't have happened at a worse time.

4-19-96

Due to our fatigue, Marty and I are never more than moments away from the next argument. I am very nervous around him because I don't want to upset him. The communication has never been worse. I feel like we might be beyond recovery. It certainly is true we can't handle any more and yet Michael hasn't come back to Santa Cruz County and is bound to be life changing and enormously stressful. At times I feel overwhelmed with sorrow and wonder how in the world everything could have fallen apart when I put so much effort into maintaining it. If I could I would quit my job, move to a smaller place alone (with the dogs), acquire a computer and spend my days writing and working on brain injury issues.

4-28-96

Marty told me he's going to rent a place for a month or two. Neither of us has used the words "trial separation," but that's what it is. There has been every indication that our separation is inevitable, but I feel extremely sad about it. I am lonely living with Marty but will probably be even lonelier when he's gone. Life seems so enormously disappointing. I regret very much that he and I are so different and so totally unable to meet each other's needs. I probably could have held up my end better if I hadn't taken the all-consuming job at the SPCA. Of course dealing with Michael's accident would bring any family down. I feel like a real loser. I think my strength and control issues make me a difficult woman to be married to.

Marty never did rent a place.

11

Walking The Plank

5-14-96

Physically I am in terrible shape. I frequently feel dizzy, like I might pass out, although I never have done so, so I'm not sure what it feels like. I am anxious and have a hard time concentrating. I am really frightened about Michael coming home and it's getting very near. I don't want to feel anxious about taking care of my own child, but I wonder if I can do all that will be required if I don't quit my job at the shelter. I wonder how I can take on another enormously tiring and stressful project when I am so screwed up. I will like the part about seeing Michael more often because I miss him. I continue to feel deep sadness about Michael's accident and the hell it has brought to him. I also miss Joe. I wish I had done more for him like paid for him to go to the dentist.

*T*he group working to set up a residential house in Santa Cruz ended up being comprised of Crystal Dunniway, Bob Ludlow, Cheryl Bentley, Steve Bennet, and myself. We all understood we were not opening a "facility" which would require licensing. We all knew we were not prepared to go through what is required to open and maintain a licensed facility. We simply aimed to have a home with people who wanted to live together. Bob Ludlow advised us that in Santa Cruz County any group of people could live together, if they chose. We would simply be renting rooms to people who wanted to live in the same house. We hoped the people in the home would eventually behave as a family, but were very naïve about how this would happen.

5-7-96

> *Things are really moving along for the group residence project. It appears Bennet will provide some funding and Bob Ludlow will sign the lease.*

For initial funding we received $10,000 from an area electronics firm, $10,000 from Michael's aunt and uncle (he is the CEO of Continental Airlines) and $10,000 from Bennet's family foundation, plus a number of smaller contributions from friends and family. It was essential to have initial starting money (seed money) because the group assumed when and if a rental house could be found, it might need modifications and almost certainly would need furnishings. We knew we would charge our residents some rent and we had a tentative budget, but it was impossible to know how it would all work out. Seed money provided some flexibility.

Once we began actually looking at houses for rent we discovered how difficult it was to find something that could accommodate wheelchairs. The problems were usually around the bathroom and the lack of a "wheel-in" shower space. In addition, most bathrooms aren't designed with room for a wheelchair user to park adjacent to the toilet so that he or she can make a transfer. Simply getting into the house can also pose a major impediment as many houses have steps to the entrance and are not ramped for a wheelchair user.

5-17-96

> *Mother and I got to see inside the lovely Victorian house at 701 Mission Street this evening. I am very excited about acquiring the house for our group residence. It is beautiful, has gorgeous windows and I think Michael would like it. It is already ramped and wheelchair accessible on the first floor (the house had previously been a coffee shop).*

Bob Ludlow knew the house on Mission Street because his law office used to be in the house next door. He found out 701 was for rent and suggested we take a look at it. The house was probably built around 1910 and was obviously a prominent Santa Cruz residence in its heyday. It was on the corner of a main street in town close to some other remarkable Victorian houses. The front porch had impressive columns and arches and the windows of the house are beveled, leaded glass. On the first floor was an extensive entrance area, parlor, living room, dining room, bathroom and kitchen. Marvelous built-in features such as window seats and an umbrella box, plus wide molding around windows, doors and the floor added to the period charm of the interior. On the second floor were three bedrooms and a bath. The house also had a full basement and a 14-space parking lot!

Once Crystal and I decided the house was workable, Bob Ludlow and I went to see the owner, an attorney in Pacific Grove. The owner was very generous and willing to allow us to rent the house for significantly under market value for a nine-month period, however, the house had some electrical problems and was missing numerous light fixtures. We would have to take care of these things ourselves. Ludlow and Bennet provided the money for the required rental deposits.

When it looked likely we would get the house Crystal and I began to make plans for moving in. We met there several times, walking around it, trying to figure out how we could make two bedrooms downstairs for Michael and Michelle, both of whom were in wheelchairs. We also had to figure out how to get a shower in the bathroom. Since the house had recently been a coffeehouse, the bathroom had only a sink and toilet. Although I was excited about the fact the house was becoming a reality, I was also dead-tired and mentally wasted. During one visit to the empty house Crystal talked to a contractor friend of hers and I lay on the floor! I also seemed to be losing my inhibitors!

We finally settled on having Michael's bedroom in what was really the front parlor of the house. The room was bright and sunny and had lovely, beveled bay windows. Michelle's bedroom would be in what was the dining room. It was a small space, but adjacent to the family area and Crystal thought Michelle would like being close to the action. This arrangement still left a considerable open area downstairs for communal family gathering. To provide a shower area we had two walls and the floor of the bathroom tiled.

The kitchen of the house was a bare skeleton since the former occupants didn't operate a full-service restaurant. There were two small cabinet units with a sink in between, so additional storage cabinets, a refrigerator and a stove would have to be acquired. We made a list of the furnishings we would need and set about contacting friends and acquaintances for donations.

A friend of my mother's was moving and she gave us her dishes, silverware, pots and pans. My mom bought the lady's sofa, upholstered chair, TV, bed, freezer and miscellaneous items. We scoured our homes for unused lamps, tables and pictures. People from Crystal's church responded by donating a stove, refrigerator, a desk, and bedding. Bob Ludlow used his advanced "wheeler-dealer" techniques to acquire a washer and dryer from a local appliance store. Family and friends helped us pick up the various donations and carry them into the house. The physical work of this was extensive and required organization and coordination to get together trucks and workers. In addition, we were coordinating workmen who were repairing the electrical problems and tiling the bathroom.

From Steve Bennet's model we knew we needed a house parent or parents to live in the house. We also knew we would need attendants. Through her church Crystal had become acquainted with a young couple who were recent immigrants from Russia. They had an infant daughter and had been living for many months in a small trailer provided for them by a local YMCA camp. Crystal approached them about their interest in possibly serving as the house parents and they responded in the affirmative. I met Sergey Nemolyaeva, Ira Shugina and their daughter, Leeza, for the first time at Bob Ludlow's office. They impressed me as sincere and conscientious and they didn't flinch when I described Michael's condition and the fact he was openly homosexual. I don't know if it was at this meeting or soon after I found out Ira had completed all her medical training and was a physician in Russia.

Later in the day they toured the Mission Street house and indicated they liked it. Our plan called for the house parents to be paid $600.00 a month and to be required to be on duty every night from 10:00 PM until 7:00 AM.

Bob Ludlow, who is a quadriplegic, recommended an attendant, Kenny Johnson, that he had used and I contacted Kenny. He was interested in leaving his position at a nursing home to work with us. Our plan called for attendants seven days a week in two shifts, the first from 7:00 AM to 4:00 PM and the second from 4:00

PM to 10:00 PM. Kenny knew several other people who were also interested in working at The Mission House and soon we had our attendant slots filled.

Crystal and I were aware of a county program called In Home Support Services (IHSS) which provided assistance to qualified individuals with such chores as personal grooming, shopping, meal preparation, house cleaning, and laundry. The attendants were paid by IHSS at the minimum wage. Steve Bennet told us his experience was that we needed to pay more than the minimum wage in order to attract the kind of attendant who would have the finesse, patience and creativity required to work with neurologically impaired people. Bennet made up the difference between the minimum wage and the $10.00 an hour his daughter's attendants were paid. We planned to do the same thing.

Both Michael and Michelle were recipients of Social Security at the rate of approximately $600 a month. Crystal and I planned to have both of them pay this entire amount every month for rent. We were fully aware from the first moment of embarking on this project that we would have to raise money in order to sustain the house financially. In order to seek tax-deductible contributions we needed to acquire IRS non-profit 501(c)(3) status and both Bob Ludlow and I began the formidable task of securing this. I bought a paperback book about the process and David went on the Internet to get me the papers which would have to be filed. A coversheet, which accompanied the tax documents, said it would take about 10 hours to fill out the papers and about 40 hours to learn to fill them out!

Within the first few months of opening The Mission House and before we had acquired our own non-profit status, we were fortunate in being able to go under the umbrella of an exciting local non-profit organization called The Live At Home Foundation. LAHF had been in existence for about ten years with a focus on getting ventilator-dependent people out of nursing homes and into their own homes. Our mission of providing residential group homes for neurologically impaired adults fit in with their mission nicely and we became a project of the Live At Home Foundation. We called our section The Assisted Living Project (ALP).

There is absolutely no question about the fact The Mission House was a very "thrown-together" project. Crystal and I were under the gun to get Michelle out of Winchester Convalescent Hospital and to get something together so Michael wouldn't have to go to a nursing home. We didn't have a detailed plan. We didn't have all the money together. We hadn't worked out all the operational issues about the house. It may seem that what we did was risky but we didn't see it that way. We were already facing the worst thing in having our kids in nursing homes.

In retrospect I think it was a blessing we had a deadline. Since opening The Mission House Crystal and I have talked to a number of families and non-profit organizations that want to do something similar, but they are always so bogged down in the details that nothing happens. Better to just step to the end of the plank and jump!

Michael was scheduled to come home sometime around June 7, but The Mission House wouldn't be ready for him to occupy until about June 17 or 18. Since I was extremely anxious about his coming home, I asked my doctor to recommend a two-month leave from my job, which she did.

6-4-96

I began my leave yesterday. So far the two days have been hectic with the phone ringing constantly and far too many problems to solve on my plate. Tonight we moved the furniture we bought from Jeanina to mom's house because we couldn't move it to the Mission Street house since the lease hasn't been signed. Everything is moving so fast, but is must since Michael is coming home Tuesday, June 11. I must get through all of this because we've come so far and Michael deserves to have an organized, well-thought out situation when he's home. He deserves the best!

12

Norwood

*I*n addition to trying to get The Mission House ready, I was pushing the contractor daily to finish our house remodel. My mom and I divided the tasks which had to happen to get the room furnished. She took over purchasing the bed and drapes and getting the drapes hung. I had the acquisition of a desk, TV, VCR, and towels on my list. As the room came together, I think Marty was proud of it. He had approached a client of his in the tile business about doing all of the work in the bathroom. The client had agreed and given us a very good price. While at NCS, Michael indicated he wanted the bathroom to be white with cobalt blue and we followed these instructions. In order for the wheelchair to have a "friendly" surface, we did away with the carpet and installed a synthetic flooring material which looks like wood.

As the day for Michael's homecoming approached, I grew more and more apprehensive. Realizing I would certainly have the primary responsibility for him, I wondered if I could manage helping him transfer onto the toilet, into the car, onto the bed. I wondered if he would sleep through the night and if I would hear him if he called me. Michael had always been a very private man and during his entire hospital stay I had worked to protect his privacy, ensuring I never saw him nude. Now I would be placed in the position of having to help him take a shower. I suppose I was most worried about managing Michael's occasional outbursts. I knew I couldn't "wrap" him as they had at NCS. The more I thought about all of this, the more frantic I became. I would often think of the Chinese saying, "Do what you fear." I told myself I could manage whatever I needed to.

Several days before Michael came home I decided I had to approach Marty, confess my level of fear, and ask for his assistance. For many months Marty had been into a routine of coming home for dinner and then going back to the office, often not returning home until the early hours of the morning. According to the plan, Kenny Johnson was going to be with Michael and me during the day, but he would leave at 4:00 PM. I was worried about being alone with Michael after Johnson left. I seem to be a person who doesn't need anything and indeed I have worked hard to be that person so Marty wasn't used to seeing me in a state of despair. I told him about my fear and begged him not to leave me alone at night with Michael. He was very tender, hugging me and saying he would be there to help me. He told me everything would be all right. I felt better.

Michael came home on 6-10-96. NCS was kind enough to have one of their staff members, Kevin, drive Michael and his belongings from Dixon to Scotts Valley. It was a very emotional moment when the van pulled into the driveway. I was overcome with joy at finally having the day arrive. I had made a big banner which hung on the garage saying, "Welcome Home, Michael."

Kenny Johnson was here and Kevin stayed the rest of the afternoon to help train us. Michael had an unrestricted diet, he had become continent while at NCS and he was able to handle most transfers with minimum supervision. He seemed overjoyed to be home.

Two of the first four nights Michael was home Marty left me alone with him, saying he had to go back to the office, even though he had promised in advance he would be available at home. When I emotionally told him I simply was falling apart, he told me I was overreacting. He said if I needed more help I should hire it.

After so many years and so many events, it seems strange to think of one defining moment when I knew the marriage was over, but there was such a moment. On the third night Michael was home, Marty again left. After 8:30 PM Michael went to bed. I knew I had to go to bed as soon as he did because I was so exhausted. I went upstairs to take a shower, wondering if I should do this when I was home alone with Michael and unable to hear him call. I had purchased an audio monitoring system designed for babies and had the receiver in my bedroom, but I was still too inexperienced to know for sure if I would be able to hear him.

With great haste I took a shower and put on a long, pink cotton nightgown. I took a sleeping pill, worrying I might sleep too deeply and not hear Michael. I got into bed and noticed how rapidly I was breathing. I felt totally out of control and panic-stricken. I thought, This is it. I'm having a nervous breakdown. I knew I couldn't do anything for the time being but stay at the house. I talked myself into being calmer and said to myself, I will end this marriage. My love for Marty has been so significantly damaged I can't ever regain it. The next morning I called my doctor and told her how depressed and distraught I was. She responded that people can only handle so much stress and, obviously, I had way too much. In addition to the sleeping pills and Prozac, she prescribed two weeks of Valium, which really proved helpful.

My mother did all she could to help. She made meals and delivered them. She came over to the house to wash dishes, do laundry, and interact with Michael. On Michael's fifth day home I had another emotional crisis and ended up crying uncontrollably. I called David and confessed I was falling apart. He called Joe who left his job in Mountain View and went right home to San Jose, then both of them immediately drove over to Scotts Valley. They simply took over. David spent time with Michael. Joe went to the grocery store and purchased supplies for meals, then handled both the cooking and the clean up. The guys spent the night, getting up with Michael and giving me the first full night of sleep in six nights.

When Marty came home to find this going on he seemed puzzled and irritated. We didn't talk about it.

6-30-96

The past three weeks have caused me to have the most negative feelings about Marty of our eighteen years together. During the darkest times, he simply hasn't been there. He's the king of passive resistance, means to help but is too sick, needs to go to work, is too tired, doesn't know what to do, thinks I'm over-reacting. Seeing his reaction during what is undoubtedly an extremely crucial moment in my life has caused me to lose respect for him. When the going is really tough, he's not there. I wonder about future crisis. What about if I am ill? I wonder what he would do. I have no plan about the future since I have no money, no other place to live, no energy, but something has definitely changed.

Michael is making good progress being back home. He has remembered many names and places. He told me he knew how to drive! He does well in stores and I've taken him out alone on several outings.

Since our new rental house was on Mission Street, we named it The Mission House. Michael moved in on June 22, 1996 and Michelle moved in at the end of the month.

6-30-96

On June 22 David and Joe spent the day helping to move all of Michael's things to The Mission House. Joe put up light fixtures. David made supply lists and, even though they were pooped, they spent the first night there with Michael. Every day since the 22nd I have been at the house helping Crystal get everything under control. I handled the gas and electric, water, cable TV, furnace repair, picked up the washer and dryer, hung curtains, mowed the lawn, and worked extensively on getting Michael's room together. I think it will all work out, but there is still much ahead.

After being evaluated by In Home Support Services, Michael qualified for the maximum number of hours, 278 a month. Michelle qualified for the same amount which meant there was about $1,200 available each month to pay attendants for each of them. When we added the supplement to bring the pay up to $8.00 or $10.00 an hour, we had a deficit of about $2,000 a month ($1,000 a month for Michael and $1,000 for Michelle).

My prediction that Michael would like The Mission House wasn't exactly accurate.

July 2, 1996

Today was one of the worst days ever with Michael. He and I had been sitting outside

*writing and reading poetry and all was pleas-
ant. We then wheeled up the ramp and all hell
broke loose. Michael began screaming, "I hate
Michelle." He refused to go into the house and
created a lengthy scene on the side porch. He attempted to hit and bite me. I really feel incapable of knowing how to handle this. He has been
cranky the last two days about using the bathroom and twice has taken everything off the bed
and peed on the mattress.*

Right off the bat we had issues with the attendants
and house parents because we were too inexperienced
and too exhausted to think through all the questions
and procedures. Bob Ludlow is such an optimist he
just thought we would put all these people in the house
and they would behave like a family and, in many ways
they did… just like a dysfunctional family! We had ne-
glected to work out details with the house parents and
attendants, such as who would do the shopping, how
would the shopper know what was needed, who would
do the general house cleaning, who would clean up after the residents, who would be responsible for recy-
cling and garbage, who would be responsible for the
lawn and watering, who made decisions for the residents, and who would cook and when.

In chapter one of *The Staff Chronicles,* the attendants took charge, with the result that the house parents felt totally out of the loop. They spent most of their
time upstairs, were not involved in any decisions, and
felt isolated. The tension in the house was palpable

and Crystal and I organized a house meeting so issues could be discussed. Because significant negative feeling already existed in the group, it was impossible to repair the situation. I received a call at home from one of our attendants just before she was to begin a shift. She said she was quitting and so were two other attendants. I hung up the phone and drove to the house in order to cover the shift.

We were to have several other attendant catastrophes before we mastered the technique of interviewing prospective candidates and accurately describing the job. Eventually we defined the responsibilities of the house parents (grocery shopping, carpet cleaning, lawn maintenance, preparation of the evening meal, being present at night in case there were an emergency) and the attendants (resident laundry, cleaning up after residents, making breakfast and lunch for residents, supervision of residents.) Crystal wrote procedures and trained new attendants. In time, things settled down and began to work relatively smoothly.

Within about five months of opening, our third resident, Juvencio Muniz, moved into an upstairs bedroom. Juvencio, who is very high functioning, had a ruptured vein in his brain when he was in his early thirties. As a result, he has short-term memory loss. Because he tended to wander, his family considered putting him in a locked facility, but instead they sent him to live for a time with one of his brothers. Juvencio wanted independence but still needed some structure and assistance with items such a money management. One of Juvencio's doctors, Dr. Neil Hersch, had heard about us and brought Juvencio to our attention. We immediately liked this polite young man and he was invited to move in.

Several months after Juvencio joined us, Mission House acquired its fourth resident, Isaac Andrews. Isaac was twenty-two years old and developmentally delayed. He worked and went to the local junior college. He traveled around town on the bus and functioned quite well on his own, however, from time to time he needed guidance and supervision. Isaac loved skateboarding and building model airplanes and his upstairs bedroom ceiling was covered with hanging models.

Michael's adjustment to The Mission House was difficult. For several months he persisted in taking all the blankets, sheets and protective plastic cover off of the bed and then urinating on it. No one ever figured out why he did this, but we all talked to him about appropriately using the bathroom. In addition, we provided a portable toilet in his room and urinals. Michael was also very argumentative about showering.

8-6-96

I picked Michael up at The Mission House at 9:00 AM and took him back around 3:30 PM and then spent about two hours with him. He continues to occasionally pee on the floor and is also refusing to cooperate about taking a shower. While I was there I talked to Michael about both of these problems. I told him his brother did not pee on the floor and he did take showers, likewise his father. Michael agreed to take a shower and we got through it pretty well. There is still much to do at the house. These issues with Michael have to be solved so the attendants can work with him. As usual, I feel under pressure and concerned that I won't have things resolved when I must return to work.

Marty is not well. He's so down about his work and continues too thin. I don't know what to do. Money is also a very big problem. I guess we could never have made it if I had worked only part-time.

8-17-96

This morning we met our contractor at 9:00 AM at the Mission House and pulled up the carpet in Michael's room. He had peed on the floor so many times the carpet couldn't be salvaged. Even the wood floor underneath was saturated. We're putting down some one-foot square vinyl tiles which should be impervious to the urine. Of course, in the best case, we'd get Michael to stop this behavior.

8-18-96

I continue to see small cognitive changes in Michael: more complex sentences and artwork.

In an attempt to understand and address Michael's outbursts, I contacted Juvencio's neuropsychologist, Dr. Hersch , asking if he would be willing to evaluate Michael and consider working with him. He agreed.

Dr. Hersch, a chubby older gentleman dressed in a hounds tooth sports coat, came to the Mission House four or five times, usually speaking both with Michael and me and sometimes with staff members. He gave us a terrific idea. He said when Michael said he couldn't remember something we should say to him, "Guess." Often, Michael would guess correctly! It was amazing. Dr. Hersch also suggested we help Michael feel more comfortable at the house by putting some of his artwork in the living room. Finally, he suggested we acquire a house cat for Michael since he was very fond of animals.

We followed these suggestions with the results that Michael responded mildly. On his last two visits Dr. Hersch gave Michael a battery of neurological tests. Michael was less than enthusiastic or cooperative. In fact at some point he flatly refused to participate. Dr. Hersch noted that he thought Michael was afraid to give answers unless he was completely sure. Hersch wrote a report about Michael stating that he had major cognitive deficits and noted, for my sake, it would probably be best if he were institutionalized.

During the experience of living through Michael's injury and rehabilitation a number of people had told me I must "go on with my life." From time to time I would try to imagine how this could be done. I would envision driving up to some large, formal mental institution. It would be a granite building with the name "Norwood" carved over the portico. I would drop Michael off. After that I got stuck. Did I go shopping? Did I go out to dinner? Did I go to a movie? How did I "go on with my life?" Although I knew that the people who suggested I had a right to my own life had my best interests at heart, the advice was hollow. For myself, I knew I wouldn't have a life worth living if Michael were in an institution.

10-12-96

Michael is doing so well. His speech has improved and it has been forever since he had a behavioral outburst. When we're together he seems happy and, often, silly. I am much more confident about being with him alone.

13

Mounting Losses

O n October 19, we held a very successful grand opening, ribbon cutting, and fundraising event at the Mission House. Michael's father came from Oklahoma, his grandmother from Austin, Texas and his uncle, Gordon, from Houston. Michael's Northern California family also attended. Using the huge parking lot at the rear of the house, we put up several shade tents and organized rows of chairs underneath them. A number of friends were our guests and the mayor of Santa Cruz, Mike Rotkin, made a welcoming speech.

The owner of the house, David Sabih, cut the ribbon and presented us with a $5,000 check to buy a van with a wheelchair lift for the house. Gordon's company, Continental Airlines, provided two round-trip international tickets and two round-trip domestic tickets and we kicked off a raffle at the open house. Crystal and I had decided we would tell our kid's stories and, being fearful of speaking in public, Crystal began her talk by saying, "I would rather be cleaning toilets!" After introducing our house parents, we awarded Michael and Michelle medallions. His read, "Michael Bethune, Hero" and hers, "Michelle Dunniway, God's Gift."

November 8, 1996

We held a very successful open house on October 19. We had seventy guests and raised $7,400. Michael was absolutely charming during the event.

Marty was basically a non-participant in the open house, although he did attend the formal ceremony. I knew he didn't like public events and I knew he was concerned about my non-stop schedule and pressure. I also knew he was uncomfortable about his appearance since he had recently lost so much weight, but for the life of me I couldn't figure out any other way. Michael needed The Mission House and The Mission House needed money.

At the end of the summer of 1996 I returned to my job full-time. Michael was living at the Mission House and came to visit our Suzanne Lane home during the weekends, occasionally staying the night. The fall was agonizing for me. Marty's angry outbursts became more frequent and his moods swung up and down like a roller coaster. When he was angry, he was scary and he was always angry with my children, my parents, the neighbors, his clients, the government, and me. During October and November I moved my clothes, make-up and medicine downstairs to Michael's room and slept there.

I first experienced Marty's rage in 1984 after we had been married for three years. During all of our time together I had worked and functioned as a homemaker. I did all the grocery shopping and cooking and most of the cleanup. I did all of the family laundry and ironing. I did most of the housecleaning and much of the yard work. I planned and managed all special events such as birthdays and holidays and I was willing to do all of this until I simply wore out.

One night Marty and I were in the bedroom and I decided to mention to him that I needed some help. I hoped he would make a commitment to doing more around the house. I was sitting on the bed when I brought up my request and while I don't recall his response, I remember it was not kind or supportive. Feeling angry, I threw a bed pillow at him and, suddenly, he changed into another person, one I had never seen before. He was hysterical and out of control. He screamed and shouted the foulest profanity. He swung his arm across the top of his dresser, making the items on top fly through the room. He ranted and raved and refused to stop talking so I could speak. I wasn't exactly a stranger to arguments. My mother and I had argued a great deal during my teenage years and my first husband was a former sailor who could argue, curse and fight with the best of them, but I had never in my life been around anyone who seemed so frantic and possessed. It was truly frightening.

Marty decided to leave and, grabbing his wallet and keys, made his way down the stairs and out the front door, still shouting. When he got to his car he threw his wallet at me screaming that I had taken everything else he had so I might as well have this money. The wallet hit the sidewalk and the money flew out. I thought I couldn't let him drive in this condition so I approached the car and told him over and over again I was so sorry I had upset him. It seemed like an eternity before he calmed down and agreed to come back in the house.

My reaction to this event was to think maybe Marty had just had a terribly bad day and surely his behavior was an anomaly, but what I feared was that I had experienced my first lesson in the repercussions of wanting or needing something. I thought, You better be very careful to not trigger another explosion. I'd have to try even harder to make Marty happy and I would definitely have to forgo any thought he would be more involved with housework.

We went a number of years before I saw the beast emerge again, this time over the issue of Michael's watching a gay video. Marty and I went out and when we came home Michael was upstairs on the phone and had obviously forgotten about the video playing on the TV downstairs. Upon discovering the video, Marty immediately became a monster, screaming obscenities at Michael. This time I took Michael to a friend's house to get him away from Marty and I spent the night at a local motel. When I came home from work the next day I was ready for the ensuing battle. I took Marty on full force, yelling and using profanity and refusing to back down. It was a very long exhausting night with Marty repeatedly telling me how my family had screwed up his life. He reacted by seeming to like the enraged me. I felt as if he respected me when I screamed back, but screaming back was not my style.

I could see the requirements if I were going to stay married to Marty. I had to be very careful about what I said. I couldn't need anything. I couldn't ask for help. I couldn't be honest. Basically I was able to live under this regime until I became completely worn down after Michael's accident. There was a point at which I simply didn't have the stamina or the energy to continue the charade. As I changed, Marty became increasingly volatile, violent and threatening.

———————————

In November, 1996 following a long night of yelling, throwing objects, threats and stalking me, he came downstairs to Michael's room where I was sleeping. He turned on all the lights. He turned on the stereo full blast. He did the same with the TV and came over to the bed where I was lying, standing over me in a threatening manner and yelling profanity at me. I tried not reacting, but this often made him even angrier. When he finally allowed me to leave the bedroom, I went upstairs in order to get the cordless phone. He blocked my passage on the stairs. I was very careful to avoid touching him because I was afraid even the slightest touch would trigger his hitting or pushing me.

During the six-hour siege that occurred that night, Marty got a kitchen knife and, holding it up in the air, said, "I'm going to kill you." It seemed perfectly possible to me he might do it. He also went in our bedroom and spent long periods of time throwing things and yelling. He was totally out of control and hysterical.

I made one phone call to Michael's attorney, Bob Ludlow, but got his answering machine. I left a message that if I were killed, Marty had done it.

The next day Bob called me at work. He told me I must get out of the house. He suggested I go to the battered women's shelter. I didn't do it but I did begin to look for a place to rent so I could move out.

11-8-96

I told Marty I want a divorce and have been looking for a place to move into. I can't believe I've been the wife in two failed marriages. I certainly never wanted that and I have tried enormously in this second chance. I can't live in fear of Marty's rage. We are totally unable to communicate and I sometimes feel significantly afraid of him. Ending this is so painful I can only take it one small step at a time. Logic tells me I can't continue to live with a man I fear. I do hate and regret all the terrible things he thinks about me.

11-27-96 *(Wednesday before Thanksgiving)*

I found a small two-bedroom house to rent and signed the rental agreement on Monday. I can move in December 1. My first thought was to just surprise Marty with the information and move out on the same day because I was worried about his reaction if he knew in advance. I was worried about his reaction if I surprised him also. I worry about his reactions period! Last night there was a mellow moment and I felt like it really was the right thing to do to tell him so I said, "I found a place." He said, "I thought you stopped looking," but other than that he didn't seem upset.

After telling Marty I was moving out, I started to pack, mostly because I was very nervous and I needed something to occupy myself. On the Friday after Thanksgiving, my family came to our Thanksgiving dinner and encountered the boxes. It created a difficult situation with lots of family tension. David had a mixed drink before dinner, which was somewhat unusual. Marty was embarrassed about the boxes and later I wished I had waited until after Thanksgiving before working on any moving preparations.

At the end of the day David went with me to take Michael back to the Mission House. David seemed distracted, but I was too out of it myself to be fully tuned-in. On the way back home David told me he had just found out he had a potentially terminal illness. As my body tensed I clutched his leg and said, "Oh, David, no!" I told David how much I loved him and how I wanted him to outlive me.

As soon as we were home and walked into the door I told Marty. He fell to his knees and said to David, "I'm so sorry, man." We all hugged each other and cried. After David left I told Marty I was going to lose both of my kids.

11-29-96

Today David told me he is HIV positive. I feel devastated and very afraid. I love David so much and I simply can't lose him. I don't understand all the recent tragedy in my life and I feel certain I can't continue.

12-4-96

After receiving the news about David I felt I simply couldn't go on with the moving out plan so I canceled everything. I'm too screwed up and too unstable to face the changes moving would bring. Marty and I have been talking and things are better. It would be ironic if another tragedy brought us together.

David is composed and positive about what is ahead. I remember the first time I ever heard about this disease on a TV story about fourteen years ago. I thought, Well, at least we know about it and we can avoid getting it. I was extremely worried when I found out that David and Michael were gay, but they both assured me they would never get it. I'm having a hard time being around people who know about all our problems. I'm embarrassed to be such a tragic character. I like to be the one who is okay and under control.

Marty seemed somewhat disappointed I hadn't moved out. He told me about his plans to paint the bedroom and move the furniture.

The third Christmas after Michael's accident was spent in our Suzanne Lane house, which was certainly an improvement over being in a hospital. We all played "happy family," an unspoken "game" in which we act out the various roles that are expected of us.

12-27-96

Christmas Eve. David, Joe, Mom, Papa, Michael, Marty and I had a chili dinner and then opened too many presents, as usual. Michael did well with the event considering the general chaos. He spent the night, going to bed at 9:00 PM. Christmas Day David and Joe went to Joe's family in Gilroy. Michael, Mom, Papa, Marty and I had a very casual throw-together lunch at our house. The day went well and I took Michael back to the Mission House about 5:00 PM.

January, February, March and April were always devoured by the tax season. I had learned to keep my distance from Marty especially during this time.

4-12-97

The end of another tax season is upon us and stress reigns. Marty has worked the strangest schedule ever... evenings and late into the night over and over again. He says that he feels like something may happen to him. He looks exhausted and complains bitterly about the demands of the clients. I feel impatient and nervous when I hear about the problems over and over again, the same basic problems from the past years. I am not the compassionate listener from past years. One of the things I've needed to do throughout the entire relationship is to honestly tell Marty what I see and feel, but I have only recently begun to do this out of frustration and reduced concerns for the consequences. I'm not the sweet, supportive wife of the past. I recognize this in myself as a characteristic of falling out of love. At some point, I've had it!

4-26-97

My relationship with Marty grows more difficult and bizarre by the day. The "tax season" never ends and he continues to be gone every night, home in the early hours of the morning and in bed when I go to work. The last two Sundays he got up at 2:00 PM. He talks constantly and is driven by excuses and the need to convince himself he has done all he could. He says all his clients, including the major ones, are mad at him. He also talks of having to pay fines and Friday did pay $600 over a problem with the Employment Development Department. He also has to reimburse a client who ended up at HR Block because Marty didn't do his return to the *client's satisfaction. I have never been in such a strange situation. This isn't a marriage, it isn't a partnership, it isn't companionship, it isn't a sexual relationship, it isn't supportive, it isn't financially good, it isn't a friendship, it isn't respectful, it isn't fun, it's a totally disappointing pain in the ass.*

On June 1, 1997 I told Marty again that I wanted a divorce. I told him in as calm and as kind a way as possible. He immediately became enraged, screaming obscenities and throwing objects off of the upper level deck of the house. After this he locked himself in the bedroom for five hours. When he came out, he was again verbally abusive and told me, "I'm going over to your parents' house right now to tell them what a fucking liar you are." This was very frightening to me because my parents are elderly and could easily be psychologically or physically hurt. I called over to their house to alert them and talked to my Dad.

I told him not to answer the door under any circumstances. After twenty minutes, Marty returned to our house. He came in the door yelling. Michael asked him to stop and Marty said to him, "This is my house. If you don't like it you can go back to The Mission House." He added, "Your mother is a drug user and a liar." Fearful of what might happen next, I called the police. They arrived and asked Marty to calm down. As soon as they left, he started it again. He stood in the living room and shouted, "I'm going to burn the house down. Compare me to O.J. Simpson. I'll accost you in public. I'll be there waiting!" I asked him to stop, saying his behavior was inappropriate. He responded with "Fuck you, bitch!" I stood up and spoke loudly, "You have to stop this. I want you to leave!" He raised his hand at me and physically shoved me, causing me to lose my balance. I fell backward onto the bed.

I called the police again, but before they got to the house, he was gone. The police issued an emergency protective order (restraining order), which was served to him the next evening when he attempted to return home. I was naïve and didn't know that when a restraining order is issued the spouse is required to move out of the house. I was surprised to hear this and was relieved to know Marty wouldn't be able to come home.

It seemed to me our lives couldn't be in any worse shape. Michael was profoundly brain-injured, David was HIV positive and I had just acquired a restraining order against the love of my life. A week after Marty left, I marked our sixteenth wedding anniversary alone.

So when it was all said and done, our marriage wasn't special. We were just average people who succumbed to extraordinary stress and tragedy, like so many other families. We fit right in with the statistics. In attempting to handle the difficult, emotional things which happened, Marty and I were stripped of the ability to love and support one another. The fact life isn't fair hit us head on. Our divorce was final in December 1997.

14

Swiss Cheese

*O*ne thing that our family has learned is that nothing is for sure with a brain-injured person. Something, which is successful one time, may not work the next. Something Michael says he likes may be despised on the next encounter. This fluctuation made it very difficult to get Michael into any kind of sustained therapy.

When he was first at The Mission House I was able to arrange through his Blue Cross insurance for speech and physical therapists to visit him there. Initially he was glad to see these people and was cooperative, but after six of seven visits he would be bored and refuse to participate. Naturally this led to his not making "enough progress" which would very soon end the visits and the payments for therapy. Several months later I worked on using MediCare for Michael to go to out-patient therapy at our local Dominican Rehabilitation Hospital. This was even less successful as Michael was in denial about the fact that he needed rehabilitation.

On each visit we would have to spend time discussing the name of the facility and trying to convince Michael to go in. After three or four visits he quit cooperating with the therapists.

We are fortunate to have a terrific organization in Santa Cruz County called The Stroke Center which is part of our local junior college. The center offers speech, physical and occupational therapy, plus cooking classes. The facility has an impressive gym and art areas for ceramics and various types of painting. It took some real convincing to get Michael accepted into the program because he is lower functioning than most students, but the center agreed to take him as long as he was accompanied by an attendant. We tried going in 1996 and again in 1998, but Michael was very turned off by the name and would say, "I didn't have a stroke." He usually refused to go in the building.

I think that there are two things at work here. First, Michael's denial. It isn't uncommon for a person with a disability, especially head injury, to avoid discussing the disability, and to avoid the company of others who are disabled. This is only natural since brain injury almost always means a lowering in status for the person. They can't do what they did before. In our support group we have talked about the fact that often, head-injury survivors in our community haven't wanted to participate in activities with other neurologically impaired people.

Secondly, it's very difficult to find professional people who have the kind of experience it takes to successfully work with a head-injury survivor. Many times therapists work with clients who want to walk again or who want to improve their speech so the therapists are not required to motivate the client. With Michael most of the battle is getting him to want to work. It takes training for a therapist to have some strategies about how to approach a patient such as Michael. For example, it may help to tell Michael who he is by saying something like this, "You're a strong, young man and I know you want to walk again." Therapists need to focus on compliments, especially if the patient has low self-esteem.

In my experience in our local community, Michael has often worked with therapists who have virtually no previous experience with a severe head-injury survivor. I have learned that in therapy situations I can't just let the hospital or facility assign a therapist to Michael. Instead I have to get involved and find out through referrals who on the staff has previous experience with head-injured people, if there is one, I have to get Michael in with that person. I have also learned that Michael does better with male therapists.

1-28-97

Michael has refused to go in The Stroke Center and refused to participate in the physical therapy at Dominican. I think I have lost my ability to talk him into things. What a challenge he is!

As a way to help Michael have some productive experiences, I asked him if he would like to give haircuts at the homeless shelter. He responded that he would. Through the local beauty college that he had attended, I found Eileen Evans. Eileen, a very good-hearted person who had been down and out once herself, volunteered to assist Michael at the shelter. I was very sure that Michael wasn't really capable of giving haircuts on his own. The three of us decided to meet at the River Street Homeless shelter every other Monday at 5:30 and do haircuts for an hour. Michael was at first overjoyed with this arrangement. Each visit he and Eileen would do an average of two haircuts. The people who were the recipients of this service were very kind to Michael and very grateful…and, boy, did they look better! But after about five or six visits Michael was no longer interested and didn't want to stay the hour. We told the shelter director that we would stop volunteering for now, but hopefully we'd be back.

Our family has tried numerous activities with Michael, some are successful, some not. We've tried concerts, movies, a trip to the Monterey Bay Aquarium, piano lessons, trips to our local amusement park, coffee houses, walks in the state park, shopping, swimming lessons, attending a musical, and going to the beach using a special beach wheelchair which can go out into the water. The three things that Michael consistently likes are eating out, going to gay bars with David and Joe, and going shopping, especially going to the grocery store. I believe he likes the grocery store so much because many of the people who work there know him and are friendly to him, speaking to him by name. Our family believes that our responsibility is to create opportunities. By now we are seasoned veterans of the School of Flexibility. We try something with the idea that it may work, or it may not. Our job is to keep trying things.

In addition to searching for activities Michael would like, we have been constantly challenged by managing Michael's behavior. Once settled into The Mission House, Michael had a long period of wanting to go to his "true house." He would be delighted to go home, but testy and uncooperative about going back to The Mission House. Sometimes he would refuse to get in the truck. Sometimes he would threaten to open the door while the truck was moving, and once or twice he actually did. Sometimes he would refuse to get out of the truck once we arrived at The Mission House. Sometimes he would explode when we were going up the ramp to the house.

In addition to these behaviors, he often refused to shower and he complained repeatedly about the traffic noise at The Mission House. A very small thing could set him off and if he went into full rage he would look for things to throw. These behaviors were naturally very disturbing to all of us who interacted with Michael and I went on a search for some help. Michael's doctor suggested that he be put on a drug called Inderal which was suppose to have calming effects. The only problem was that Michael refused to take any medicine, so the Inderal had to be "hidden" in things he would drink, if we could get him to drink it! All in all, it wasn't very helpful.

In my search for help with the behavior issues, I located two local psychologists with experience working with head-injury survivors, however, I didn't really feel that either one of them had a grip on Michael. Both of them seemed puzzled by what he did and neither had confident answers about what we could do. One attempted to do a neuropsychological exam on Michael but he was generally unsuccessful because Michael was very uncooperative. During their last session Michael slammed doors and screamed leading the examiner to conclude that Michael was very uncomfortable being evaluated and that he would disengage rather than provide educated guesses. The psychologist recommended "that Michael work with a mental health professional both to control explosive behaviors and also to more fully assess the range of psychological and neuropsychological functions. It would be ideal if Michael could be placed in a facility specializing in this clinical activity."

I met the second psychologist in his office. I described Michael's behaviors and he basically said, "Um, well, let me see" and "Yes, I can see that he is difficult" etc. I left the meeting with nothing new.

At last someone suggested to me that I talk to Lauranel Rose, an occupational therapist that owns and operates a for-profit residential group home for traumatic brain-injured adults called Rose Hill. I knew Lauranel because I had visited Rose Hill and asked her questions as part of setting up The Mission House. I called her and asked her if she would consider consulting with me and, to my great relief, she agreed. Lauranel understood Michael's actions, could describe why he did what he did and she made suggestions about what we could do. The suggestions didn't require physical intervention so usually one person could handle the situation alone. I think that Lauranel was so helpful because she had actually lived with brain-injured people and her suggestions were practical.

Lauranel, a petite blond, came to The Mission House on several occasions, first to observe Michael and secondly, to conduct a couple of workshops for the attendants. Her techniques involved ignoring Michael when he complained over and over again about the same things and rewarding his appropriate behavior by allowing him to go home or to have special privileges. If he had a major outburst at Mission House he was required to go into his room until he was calm. If needed, the attendant would pull the wheelchair backward into the room and lock Michael in there for a few minutes. These techniques helped substantially and basically made it possible for Michael to stay at Mission House.

6-22-97

Michael has had major outbursts last week at Mission House and the residents and attendants are ready to revolt. They want him gone. This week I'll bring him home every night just to give them a break. It'll really be hard on me, but it feels like there is no other solution. I hope this works.

8-20-97

Yesterday was the second workshop with Lauranel. When she talks everything seems logical and simple, but in no time I feel buffaloed again by Michael's behavior.

8-25-97

I successfully got Michael in for a blood test today. Instead of being so bummed out about what I can't get him to do, I realize I should concentrate on the wins.

For many months Michael was very content at home. He played ball with our three dogs, painted, sat out on the patio in the sun and seemed to relish being back in his childhood home. But eventually, he became bored and irritable. He wanted me to take him someplace all the time. He wanted us to have lots of company. He wanted to go out at night. Usually I could keep things calm enough so that a full-blown outburst didn't occur, but not always.

Because Michael's room in on another level I wasn't able to roll him backwards into his room when he was inappropriate. On several occasions I left him alone in his room while he was having an outburst, but he did quite a bit of damage throwing things. Sometimes I could appeal to him by telling him that he wouldn't be allowed to come back home if he continued to be abusive.

3-38-98

I picked Michael up at Mission House this morning and we drove up Highway 1 to Davenport and had lunch at the Cash Store. The coast was beautiful. We got home about 1:45 PM. A skunk had sprayed Woody (our dog) at midnight the night before and I told Michael the house smelled badly before we arrived. As soon as we got in the house I told Michael that I needed to wash Woody to try to get the odor off of him. I took Woody into Michael's shower.

While I was in there I heard the sound of glass breaking. I opened the bathroom door to find that Michael had thrown his mirror and was in a full-blown rage apparently over the odor. He had me trapped in the bathroom. He struck out at me several times, succeeding in grabbing my clothing. He picked up other items to throw and I would wrestle him for them.

Just as I succeeded in getting Michael slightly calmer, my mother arrived as she had plans to take Michael to the movies. She was quickly angered at what she saw and she decided to do back to Michael whatever he did. This approach resulted in his being fully enraged again. Things seemed so out of control that I decided I needed help.

I called 911 and the Scotts Valley Police quickly arrived. Michael calmed down, but I felt so concerned that I knew he couldn't stay at our house. I asked the police to take him to the psychiatric unit of Dominican Hospital. I accompanied Michael over there. The crisis intake person told me that they probably wouldn't take Michael because they had three criteria and he had to meet one of them. The criteria were, he was dangerous to himself, he was dangerous to others, or he was unable to care for himself. I said, "Well, we have two out of the three."

I asked the intake person where else Michael would go. I said that jail absolutely would be inappropriate. The intake person said he didn't know, but he didn't think they took head-injured people. He agreed to call the supervisor who, fortunately, responded that they did. Once Michael was in the door of the hospital, I decided to leave because I believed that he would be all right and I thought that the experience would be more poignant for him if he were alone.

After about five hours I was able to talk to the psychiatric nurse. I told her that I was willing to come and get Michael if he would agree to going to The Mission House. In addition, he had to willingly agree to take medication for anger control. She talked to Michael and reported that he was very remorseful and had agreed to the conditions. I drove over to the hospital and was admitted to one of the patient/family gathering areas. While I was there one of the crisis counselors told Michael that what he had done was very serious and that if he came back to the psychiatric unit, he would be required to stay a full seventy-two hours. He told Michael that he was in a locked mental health unit. He told him he was now classified as a "51-50," a person with mental disabilities. Michael seemed very sobered by all of this.

About two weeks after this event my mother and I attended a three-day workshop presented by Dr. Harriet Zeiner called Building A Life After Brain Injury. The workshop was terrific in that it gave us renewed hope in managing Michael's behavior. Zeiner introduced the idea that a disabled person can't get rid of the disability, but, they can be a smart disabled person by learning compensatory behaviors. If the person doesn't want to do this, then, in effect, they "choose" to behave like they are crazy. For example, because Michael has problems with anger control he can learn when he is first becoming angry to say, "Because I have problems with anger control, I need to take a break to cool off." She calls this joining of a specific problem with a specific solution a "construct." Another construct for Michael might be, "because I have problems remembering, I write dates down in my organizer."

Zeiner also talked about the "sandwich" technique of putting a criticism in between two compliments such as, "Michael, you are such a good-looking guy that I bet you'd like to comb your hair before we go out. I know you always like to look your best."

Another concept, which Zeiner introduced, was that the brain after a major injury is like Swiss cheese, there is much that is "good" and intact, but there are also "holes" where cells have died. The holes represent deficits. The traumatic brain injury survivor is not crazy. They are not retarded and they do not have a mental illness. What they have are deficits from brain injury.

I got a piece of Swiss cheese and showed it to Michael. We talked about the concept and about the fact that he has much good brain material left and that where there are holes, he must develop ways around them. He was calm and cooperative during this conversation and understood. Of course, since Michael has such impaired memory, I couldn't be sure he would remember the conversation.

I took the information from the Zeiner workshop and condensed it down to the things that I thought would be helpful in working with Michael and I gave a one-hour review to the attendants at The Mission House. I put a simple schedule together for Michael since Zeiner said that a routine makes it easier for brain-injured people because they have less to remember. I put together a very simple organizer for Michael to use and I bought some "brain-builder" games (tan gram, geoboard) which Zeiner had suggested.

April 22, 1998

Yesterday Dr. Quinn had a last minute cancellation and I was able to get in to see him at 10:30 A.M. I talked to him about Michael's recent outbursts and my interest at looking at drugs that might be helpful. I also told him that Michael had recently been walking up and down the ramp at Mission House, using the rail for support.

I asked the doctor if he would write orders again for Michael to go to P.T. He responded that he thought Michael should go to a residential be-havior modification program and live there for six or nine months. He said he knew of a good one in Ontario, California and that he thought they took MediCare. I wrote down the name and said I would call. Meanwhile I tried to fight off the messages I was getting from my brain that none of these places take MediCare and, if they do, they have a waiting list of several years for the one or two slots.

I asked Quinn what he thought of the Mental Health Unit at Dominican Hospital and his reaction to having Michael go there if the outbursts continued. He said that it was a good place and he thought that it would be very educational and sobering for Michael to be admitted there.

After the appointment I went by The Mission House and took Michael out to lunch at our favorite place, the China Szechwan. When we got back I asked him to write a brief note in his organizer about what we had done. He asked me why he should do this and I said, "Because you have problems remembering, writing down what happened will help you know more about your life." That did it! Michael was mad. He threw the organizer book and then moved to the table, threw a chair over and pulled the tablecloth off. I grabbed a flower vase that was on the middle of the table, holding it for the next minutes while I tried to prevent him from doing further damage. We ended up outside on the ramp where I was trapped in a corner. Michael hit me and grabbed my arm, squeezing and bruising it. In an effort to defend myself, I set the vase down on top of the ramp rail. In a flash Michael picked it up and threw it. I called to Crystal and asked her to call 911.

It seemed like an eternity before the Santa Cruz Police arrived. When they finally did, I briefly explained the situation and asked them to take Michael to the mental health unit at the hospital. The officer explained to me that he couldn't do that because he hadn't seen the outburst. He said Michael would have to admit himself. I explained that Michael is an incompetent adult and that I am his guardian. No matter. Michael would have to voluntarily admit himself. I left Michael with the police and went into call Dr. Quinn to see if he would admit Michael. While I was in the house the police talked Michael into going. This was probably possible because Michael likes men and these guys were young and handsome. So we were off to "Norwood."

Once we arrived at the Mental Health Unit, the police left and I was soon faced with the same crisis intake worker we had seen before. He told me that they were very busy and that there was another person ahead of us and the wait would be about 1 ½ to 2 hours. I told the worker that Michael did not wait well and a wait of this length might bring about an outburst. I asked to speak to a supervisor and, at that, the worker agreed to get back to us sooner.

We waited over an hour before a tall, frowning psychiatrist approached me in the lobby. He asked me why we were there and when I told him he said, "you can't just drop him off here." His callus statement incensed me. I asked the doctor what I was supposed to do and he said, "can't you take him to the regional center?" I explained that the regional centers provided marvelous services, but only for people who are developmentally delayed (retarded). They offered nothing for brain injury survivors. I stated that I would not take Michael back home now because I felt afraid of him. I also would not take him back to The Mission House because everyone there was afraid of him. The doctor said, "well, you can't abandon him here." I responded that I had no intention of abandoning Michael. That I had been at this for quite awhile and absolutely had no plan to abandon him. The doctor asked how I planned to pay for the hospitalization and I produced Michael's Blue Cross and MediCare cards. Briskly and without smiling, the doctor took them to the business office, leaving us alone in the lobby.

Michael said, "I don't want to stay here" and began to move toward the door. When I stopped him, he flew into another rage, but this time the doctor could see him from the window of the office. Michael pounded on the glass doors and screamed. Eventually three security people arrived, plus several staff people. The doctor came out and said, "We'll admit him."

Michael sat facing the door surrounded by a circle of people. There was a long moment of silence and finally I said, "Michael no one here is going to hurt you.

We're all on your team and want to help. We need you to go into the hospital." He said, "Okay," turning his chair around and wheeling beyond the door into the locked portion of the facility.

The doctor then invited me into his office to get a brief history. He was a very different man than the one I had talked to initially in the lobby. He said, "This must be very difficult" and I responded, "Yes." He told me that there were some very good new drugs and asked if I would be willing to try Michael on them and I agreed. I left the hospital about 4:30 P.M. in the afternoon and drove over to The Mission House to let them know what had happened. Crystal, Ira and Sergey were all very sorry, but they all thought that the hospitalization experience might be good for Michael.

I went home and called Marty. I asked him to come over and spend an hour with me and he did. It was a really good time together. We laughed and reminisced and talked about how dreadfully difficult life is and we hugged each other.

Michael spent four days and nights at the Mental Health Unit. While there he was started on two new drugs, Valium and Depacote, a mood leveler. When he came home he was very confused and I had to take him out to the mailbox to prove to him that we were at his house. I pored over the information on the new drugs and discovered that a negative side effect of Valium is confusion, so I stopped the medication. Michael also left the hospital without bladder control. Initially I thought that this was also because of the Valium and the resulting confusion which may have made it difficult for him to remember where the bathroom was. After several days of the continuing incontinence, I looked carefully again at the drug information and found out that a side effect of Depacote is loss of bladder control. The brochure lists a number of side effects and says, "if you are bothered by these effects, contract you doctor." I wondered who wouldn't be bothered by lack of bladder control! I took Michael off of the Depacote. It was a week before he returned to his "normal" cognitive functioning, but the hospital stay definitely had a sobering effect on Michael. He knew he had been in a mental hospital and he knew he didn't want to go back.

15

The Insurance Company Is In Charge

There are a number of themes throughout this book concerning our struggle with the tragedy of Michael's accident, including how we managed his twenty-two months of hospitalization, what happened to our interpersonal and family relationships, and what we learned about the politics of hospitals and insurance companies. No part of our experience was more continually frightening and frustrating than dealing with the insurance company.

As a part of writing this book I decided that I had to do the research to get my arms around what was going on because, ultimately, the insurance company has so much power over the injured person and the family. It can make or break your life. I suspected that much of what I would learn I wouldn't like and neither would readers of the book. However, I think most people are empowered by knowing, even if the information makes them angry.

Throughout Michael's hospitalization and rehabilitation, I felt as if a terrible, large, nebulous creature controlled his life, and therefore ours. This creature seemed to govern how long Michael was in a certain hospital and whether or not he received therapy. The creature decided when Michael had made "enough" progress. Initially I had a very poor idea of the composition of the creature. I knew it had a tendril called the hospital case manager and one called the insurance company case manager. I knew it had a part called the doctor and one called the hospital and one called the insurance company. At first I felt too overwhelmed to try to figure it all out. I would ask a question and get a small glimpse of the creature, but for years it remained steeped in ambiguity, by design, I think. So here are some facts that may be helpful to the next person making this awesome journey.

The Power of Insurance Companies

In 1979 the Los Angeles Times reported that the insurance industry collected annually nearly $150 billion in insurance premiums, an amount which represented approximately one-eight of the total disposable income of all Americans (LA Times, July 15, 1979, IV, at 1, col.5). This alone gives the industry significant power. None of us "negotiates" with the insurance company. None of us has any bargaining power with the company. We simply glance through the policy, adhere to the sign-up and premium requirements and rest assured that we are "covered." In fact, the insurance contract is called a "contract of adhesion" because one party makes all the rules and the other party adheres. All is well in this happy scenario until you have a claim.

As early as 1910 the California court noted:

> *"It is matter almost of common knowledge that a very small percentage of policy-holders are actually cognizant of the provisions of their policies and many of them are ignorant of the names of the companies issuing the said policies. The policies are prepared by the experts of the companies, they are highly technical in their phraseology, they are complicated and voluminous... and in their numerous conditions and stipulations furnishing what sometime may be veritable traps for the unwary."* -- Raulet v. Northwestern Ins. Co., 157 Cal. 213, 107 P. 292 (1910).

No family dealing with the severe injury of a loved one is capable of taking on the insurance company. Maybe you think that the hospital case manager will help you, and, if you are lucky, you may have a sophisticated person who will help, but it is more likely that the case manager is overworked. Rarely does this person have the time or training to keep up with changing insurance policy rules and billing requirements. My advice for families dealing with severe injury cases is to consult an attorney, the earlier the better.

One reason for this is that stunned family members are not equipped to wade through the standard insurance responses such as "certain care may not be covered" or "the procedure is not medically necessary" or "enough progress has not been made," fighting a legalistic battle when they are already involved in the most traumatic event of their lives.

Sandy S. McMath, a Little Rock, Arkansas attorney whose practice emphasizes damage recoveries for head and spinal cord injury victims, has written that "one cold statistic, empirical but precise, is that of a thousand policyholders 'erroneously' denied benefits, 90 percent never consult an attorney." Consult an attorney, even if you have no idea how you're going to pay for it. Most attorneys will provide the first consultation at no charge.

How to Find the Right Attorney

I found Michael's attorney through our local support group called Caregivers to Brain-injured Adults. If you don't have a support group in your area, look for an advocacy group for the disabled or a center for independent living and ask people there for a referral. There is probably a center for disabled students at your local junior college and this is another possible resource.

When you have identified the attorney and made an appointment, go through these questions at your first meeting:

- Are you experienced in analysis of insurance health and liability policies?
- Do you handle personal injury cases?
- Are you experienced in special needs trusts?

- Are you experienced in lien subrogation (reimbursement)?
- Do you have knowledge of public benefits?
- Do you have experience with medical resources?

Remember that this attorney isn't just interviewing you. You are interviewing him or her and if you don't feel comfortable with the person or the answers, go on to the next name on your list. You will feel a sizable sense of relief once you have found the right attorney.

What the Law Requires in a Medical Emergency

Most of the federal law (Title 42, U.S.C. section 1395dd) and that of the state of California (Health and Safety Code sections 1317 through 1317.9a) deals with requirements of emergency departments and are designed to prevent "dumping" of medically indigent patients during an emergency. In fact, the California code states that "emergency services may not be based upon, or affected by, a person's insurance status, economic status or ability to pay for medical services.

These services must be rendered without first questioning the patient or any other person regarding the patient's ability to pay for treatment. Payment information may be obtained after services are rendered."

My observation was that during the acute hospital stay, everyone gets the same treatment, intensive care, MRIs, specialists, therapy, the works and this observation seems consistent with what the law says about treating people in an emergency.

When the Emergency Is Over

Once the acute hospital stay is over, everything else is based on insurance or the ability to pay privately. In cases of serious injuries, as soon as possible patients leave the acute hospital and go to a sub-acute facility. When they are medically stable, they are transferred from the sub-acute to a rehabilitation hospital. When rehab is over they go home or, if that isn't possible, they go to a nursing home.

People with money may be able to hire staff and stay at home or pay privately for upgraded institutional care. People without insurance have no choice, they go to the county hospital for rehab. Those who have Medicaid may be able to get into various rehabilitation hospitals, but often these facilities have a very limited number of Medicaid beds (one or two).

Hospitals would rather not have Medicaid patients because they are paid less for their services. The best possible circumstance is if the injured person was hurt on the job and was covered by Worker's Compensation. These people are in the best position to get everything, the best hospitals and longer stays and even long-term residential care.

Laws That Govern Hospital Transfers

First, it is important to realize that each step down-ward in the process from the emergency intensive care unit ($10,000+ a day) to the sub-acute hospital to the rehabilitation hospital represents a decrease in cost to the insurance company. So, as you can imagine, insurance practices and policies are established with the goal of quickly moving the patient from one level to the next.

What the law does require when a patient is transferred from one hospital to another is that "the patient's physician determine that such a transfer or discharge would not create a medical hazard to the patient." Notice that it does not require that the transfer be in the best interest of the patient. The law also requires that "the patient or the person legally responsible for the patient has been notified, or attempts have been made over the 24-hour period prior to the patient's transfer and the legally responsible person cannot be reached."

With those scant guidelines and under pressure from the insurance companies, each hospital develops its own policy on transfers. Generally these policies will involve obtaining the consent of the patient to be transferred, including an explanation of the need for the transfer and of the alternatives to such transfer. The hospital may have a "Refusal of Transfer Form" for the patient or family to sign if the transfer is refused. The hospital will likely provide a transfer summary to the next facility, including the "rehabilitation potential" of the patient.

Once a decision has been made to transfer someone, the transferring hospital is under the gun to accomplish the transfer as soon as possible because any delay in effecting the transfer could result in the denial of payment by the insurance company for the patient's additional stay.

The Decision to Transfer a Patient

Once the emergency crisis is over, a person at the hospital called a "case manager" must negotiate regularly with a "case manager" at the insurance company in order to keep the patient at the hospital. Usually extensions are given for only a few days at a time, or in the best case, a week or so. Insurance company application forms include a number of ambiguously worded phrases which are used to deny longer stays, phrases such as "certain care may not be covered," "the patient must make significant practical improvement in a reasonable period of time," and "coverage stops when further progress toward the established goal is unlikely." If the hospital can't prove to the insurance company that the patient needs to be there, then the insurance is going to stop paying. Several people who have been in rehabilitation hospitals have told me that they were greatly pressured by being told daily that they had to make progress.

The Hospital Works for the Insurance Company

It dawned on me during Michael's rehabilitation that, in reality, the doctors and therapists and the hospitals work for the insurance company. The insurance company pays the bills. I think the alliance between the doctors, therapists, hospitals and the insurance company is a very unsatisfactory one for medical professionals, but they are trapped in the system. Despite their efforts to remain professional, I have heard enough comments by medical staff to know that they aren't comfortable with what happens to patients. Some people leave the profession because of these ethical issues. It takes a high level of sophistication, and precious time and energy on the part of the hospital to defeat the insurance companies' goal of discharging the patient as soon as possible.

One well-known rehabilitation hospital realized that their case managers had to educate the insurance companies' case managers about head injury and the steps to recovery. The team would spend time during rounds discussing how to justify keeping the patient. Therapists set up programs specifically so that progress could be achieved and reports provided to the insurance company were developed to document the subtlest changes in the patient. Video tapes were provided to the insurance company and, in a new program, patients who have been out of the hospital for several months are filmed so that the insurance company can see the they continued to improve.

As a patient's time in the hospital increases, it is more and more difficult to justify progress and more effort must be spent with the insurance company. If a person with a head injury is walking, it is almost impossible to justify keeping him or her because walking seems to be the criterion that indicates a person is back to normal. Actually, many head-injured patients who are walking are in no condition to be discharged from the hospital because they may suffer from memory loss, confusion, inability to communicate, agitation or a number of other traumatic brain injury complications (one case manager I encountered called them "the walking wounded"). Michael got to stay in the acute rehabilitation hospital for nine months because of the condition of his legs. The insurance company's position is that cognitive progress can be done on an outpatient basis. Of course, this is far less expensive for the insurance company than hospitalization. The problem is that few medical professionals or families agree with this argument.

When You Refuse A Transfer

I asked one case manager what happens when the family has been told that the patient must be discharged or transferred and the family refuses to take action. I was told that the hospital issues a Letter of Denial in which they state that the patient will not be covered by insurance after a certain date and that payment will become the private responsibility of the family. If the family abandons the patient at the hospital, the hospital will work in concert with county agencies in order to accomplish transferring the person to a nursing home, something they have the legal right to do.

Special Problems with Head Injury

Head injury is a very new field for insurance companies because ten to fifteen years ago people with severe head injuries simply didn't live. New techniques, including helicoptering the victims to trauma centers and the use of intercranial pressure monitors, have resulted in saving some lives, but insurance companies have remained very uninformed about catastrophic injuries and are not prepared when the severe head injury case hits their desk. They use general rehabilitation guidelines written by Medicare for injuries such as a broken hip, recovery from a stroke or a fractured ankle. There are no guidelines written for head injury, a condition which may require considerable time and therapy to see improvement. The lack of guidelines specifically for head injury works to the advantage of the insurance company since recovery is often very slow, making it difficult for the hospital to continually prove "significant improvement in a reasonable amount of time."

The End of the Line

"Custodial Care" is the term applied to the type of services provided by nursing homes. People who receive custodial care are not expected to improve and the goal of the care is to simply provide basic services such as meals, medication management, bathing, and supervision. Insurance companies don't pay for "custodial care" in nursing homes, unless the patient has Medicaid. The courts have said that the purpose of medical insurance is to restore someone to health and, when that can't happen, the insurance has no more responsibility. Even though Medicaid will pay for nursing homes, these facilities generally don't want to accept young people with severe head injuries because they are often a very heavy care burden and the long-term placement isn't financially beneficial to the corporation. In addition, often nursing homes have little or no experience with a severely head-injured person and therefore, don't know how to care for them. However, for most families this is the only choice unless there has been a settlement providing funding to pay $6,000 or more a month for upgraded institutional care or private at home care.

What Can You Do?

What can you as a family member do? First, get your injured loved-one into the very best, most sophisticated rehabilitation hospital that you can find. Before you agree to the admission of your loved one, ask the case manager what strategies the hospital uses to justify keeping the patient. This is critical because the ability of the hospital to hang on to your loved one may make a big difference in their eventual recovery. Ask the facility how many patients they have had with your loved one's injury in the past year. Experience with a specific injury is very important not only in providing the best care for your loved one, but also in being able to educate the insurance company.

The family must also make themselves known to the insurance company. Find out who the insurance case manager is and call this person. Introduce yourself and tell them that you represent your loved one. Tell the case manager what you want and expect. Request copies of all correspondence between the insurance company and the hospital. According to Bob Ludlow, there is no such thing as insurance company/hospital privilege and you have the right to see any and all information released on your loved one. Keep in touch with the insurance company case manager. Ask for a copy of whatever rehabilitation guidelines are being used (it will probably be the Medicare General Rehabilitation Guidelines). If you can't get them from the insurance company, try to get them from the hospital. You want to see these because they carry so much weight.

Get involved with the treatment team. There should be weekly updates on your family member that you are entitled to see. In addition, you are entitled to a meeting with the treatment team periodically. Take a tape recorder to these meetings, and always behave reasonably in order to avoid being labeled as a "problem family."

Of course, no matter what you do, at some point the hospital can't hold on to the patient any longer and you will be notified of a discharge date. In most hospitals "discharge planning" begins early in the stay and is another fearsome future event. In fact, insurance companies are demanding that hospitals begin discharge planning earlier and earlier.

If the hospital tells you that your loved one is going to be transferred to another facility, be aware that the hospital's policy may allow you to receive complete information and explanations concerning the needs for and the alternatives to the transfer. Ask to see the full hospital policy on transfers. Also be aware that if the hospital tries unsuccessfully to contact you for twenty-four hours, they can transfer your loved one without consent.

Options to Nursing Homes

The medical model favors nursing homes for a severely disabled person and seldom sees any other way of providing care. All of us must work to defeat the "in and quickly out" insurance plan which puts monetary considerations ahead of anything else. We need to become informed, write letters to the editors of our local papers, contact our elected officials, make a stink. Here's a sobering tale. In May, 1998 a twenty-six year old quadriplegic who lived in Santa Cruz apparently was successful in having Dr. Jack Kevorkian assist him in suicide. The newspaper story told of a short and inadequate rehabilitation, a lack of counseling, an inability to get the basic equipment he needed and pressure to put Matt Johnson in a nursing home.

When I see something like this in the paper, I write a brief letter to the editor about how the system must be changed. I also save these kinds of stories to include in letters to elected officials in order to prove my point that our medical delivery system is frightening. It is, after all, in the best interest of each of us to try and effect change since we never know when we will be the next victim of the system.

The other thing we have to do is defeat the nursing home lobby which has an exclusive hold on anyone who, for a variety of medical reasons, can't live at home. The money that the government is willing to spend to support people "living" in nursing homes should be available for people to hire attendants so that they can stay in their own homes or for them to join a group living situation. Today, because of the way the law is structured, this isn't possible.

Reform is needed so that the disabled or elderly person can choose where they live. From a financial standpoint, the "live at home" option makes sense. For example, Medicaid will pay $4,000 a month for a person to live in a nursing home and much of that expense goes to overhead and administration. If a person had this $4,000 a month, or even less, they could hire attendants and receive direct care. Living at home is, obviously, more normal, more nurturing, more comfortable, more supportive, and more humane.

The population of the United States is growing older. In addition, medical technology is saving more and more people who have extensive medical needs, such as severe head injury victims and infants with significant congenital disabilities. It is hard to imagine that any one of us won't be touched at some time in our life by the "nursing home issue." Now is the time to express our dissatisfaction to our elected officials and make the kind of noise required to change the system.

16

Making a New Fabric

*A*s I conclude this book we are more than four years post trauma. Bob Ludlow and Michael Moore pursued a lawsuit in Michael's behalf against the State of California after their investigation revealed that 110 accidents had occurred at the site of the crash. They discovered that the state had been aware for some time that road improvements were needed. The case is scheduled to go to trial in January, 1999.

As you might imagine, everyone in our family has been profoundly changed by our experience. As part of writing this book I asked each person in the family to answer three questions: how has Michael's accident changed their life, what they had learned from going through this experience and how they would rate it against other traumatic experiences in their life?

David said that the accident changed his life by strengthening his ties to the family. He now has a clear knowledge of how much the family means to him and things involving the family have a higher priority for him. For example, David had been an exchange student in Spain when he was fifteen, returning to the Canary Islands for nine months when he was twenty-two. He had always thought that someday he would live in Spain. Now he knows that he never will because he wants to be near Michael. Perhaps the most difficult change for David has been in his relationship to Michael. The two of them were very close and people often noted that, when they were together, they didn't even notice other people. They talked to each other incessantly. The brother that David knew is gone now and David's new brother requires supervision, direction, assistance, and unending patience.

As to what he learned from the experience, David responded that, through his research, he learned a great deal about the brain and brain injuries. He learned that the world is made for normal people and that brain injury is a significant hidden epidemic in this country. He developed increased sensitivity for people who are disabled. He learned about the connection between people with neurological deficits, the homeless and our penal system. In this scenario a person who is brain-injured or mentally impaired, dressed and ambulatory is often abandoned by mental health agencies to "make it on their own." Frequently these people are unable to hold a job, function in society, control their behavior, advocate for themselves or seek assistance, so they become homeless.

If they have anger control problems and difficulty understanding the consequences of their actions, it isn't a big leap to understand how they get into problems with the police which lead to their induction into the penal system. Joan Petersilia, Professor of Criminology, Law and Society at the University of California, Irvine, has conducted research which indicates that about 50,000 prisoners in the United States, or 4% of all inmates, suffer some form of mental deficiency.

Finally, David learned that the severely injured person must have an advocate who will press for what is needed and what is right. In retrospect he saw how our family assumed various roles and he realized that the family must be allowed to work through the process of dealing with the tragedy. There is no right answer or set formula.

As to rating this experience with others in his life, David believes that our experience is the most difficult medical experience that any family can have. Even with terminal illness, there is death, grieving and eventual acceptance. With severe brain injury there is no end, no closure. I should add that, despite the difficulties. David is very glad that his brother lived.

I saw David grow up when Michael had this accident. Prior to it, David was sometimes thoughtless, overly assertive and self-centered. Overnight he became a considerate, supportive, reliable and kind family member. He also became my best friend.

Joe responded to the questions by saying that he, too, now places increased value on the family. He said that he was moved by the way our family pulled together, putting as many extraneous things as possible aside. He told me that in the beginning, he knew he could bail out of the relationship with David because it wasn't long-standing, and, in addition, he had a hint of what was ahead. However, he made the choice to stay in order to support David. Doing that meant a significant shift in their relationship as David focused on Michael for extensive periods of time.

Joe said he learned much about what can be gained by a family working as a team, sticking together, communicating and assigning duties. Joe had experienced the death of several special people in his life, but he said this was different because Michael survived with profound injuries and there really was no closure.

My father told me that his life was changed significantly by the accident because of my mother's extensive involvement which required her to be gone a lot. He said he is more afraid of cars and worries more about accidents. He realizes now that catastrophic accidents can happen to anyone and are more common than he thought. He said, "Life is pretty uncertain." In rating this experience against others, he replied that along with the death of his three brothers, this was the most difficult thing in his life.

My mother had her carefree retirement days abruptly ended by Michael's accident. Her priorities changed overnight as she dedicated herself to becoming a primary caregiver. Her physical and mental capacities were significantly stretched during a time in her life when she expected to travel and play bridge. My mother learned a great deal about brain injury, acute hospitals, rehabilitation hospitals, therapy, and insurance. She learned to be very grateful for the smallest improvement Michael would make. She began to look at others who are disabled with more compassion. She realized that "invisible injuries" such as brain trauma cause the average person to feel uncomfortable because they know so little about the brain. She often felt without social support because Michael's injury was so demanding, so mysterious and unending.

As for me, I learned that prolonged tragedy strips away pretense within the family, even when it has been carefully constructed over a number of years. Ultimately fear, weariness, frustration and burnout work to leave each person involved naked. Standing with my family in this most primitive condition I discovered a group of people who, because of their great caring, I respected, loved, admired and forgave. Because of Michael's accident, we now truly know each other.

I learned to be a more sensitive person. In the past I had always felt concern for those who were disabled, disenfranchised, homeless, abused, etc., but, other than animals, I never really did anything. Now I am actively involved in work regarding housing for the disabled as well as insurance and prison reform. My life feels more meaningful. In some ways I think I have become a sage. Having survived something so difficult, my work now is to help others who are behind me in the journey.

I learned to do what I fear. The gravity of the situation required that I put fear aside and step out. Perhaps this was the greatest lesson of all. If something worked or went well, I celebrated. If it didn't, I learned to let go and focus on the next task at hand. I realized that I didn't have the power to fix everything and for a goal-oriented person like me, this was very hard. I figured out that my role was to be creative, provide opportunities, explore options and advocate. I no longer tied my self-worth to the success of every project.

Everything that happened to me in my life prior to Michael's accident was just a dress rehearsal for dealing with his severe brain injury. I learned to appreciate all the adversity I had overcome in my life, all the demons I had slain, and all the business experiences I had. I was tougher and wiser because of them. I was a better negotiator. I was more realistic and reasonable. I was more mature.

And about that issue of ever being happy again, I am happy. It took a long time. I didn't "get over it," instead, as a dear friend suggested, I wove the tragedy and loss into the fabric of my life. Today it takes less for me to be happy. I am happy because Michael had a good day and the sun is out. I am happy because flowers are blooming in my yard. I am happy because I am a confirmed survivor.

And what about Michael? Today Michael is standing and working on walking. His vocabulary continues to become more and more sophisticated and he is beginning to read, using a ruler to underline the sentence. He is twenty-six years old and he wants a job, money, a car and a partner, just like any other twenty-six year old. He may never have any of these things so he is often frustrated. Minute by minute he battles anger control issues, losing sometimes, but, more often, gaining control.

He spends his days at The Mission House listening to music, painting and conversing with other residents.

In addition, he does chores such as dishes, folding laundry or starting a load of laundry in order to earn spending money. He still requires twenty-four hour a day supervision, but his life is rather rich. He goes out into the community almost every day. He goes to concerts, movies and enjoys eating out. He is learning compensatory strategies such as saying to someone, "I'm sorry, but I need to be reminded of your name." He sells his artwork to benefit the homeless in Santa Cruz County, which enables him to have the positive feeling of helping others.

Not long ago I was talking to Michael and he said to me, "Mom, I have an excellent life."

Epilogue

2005 finds me as Michael's conservator and the trustee of the monies we received from the suit against the State of California. Investigation into the scene of the accident proved that other serious accidents had occurred at this sight and that the state knew the area to be dangerous. Following two separate negotiation sessions with state attorneys, I agreed to accept an out-of-court settlement of $4,500,000. Michael's attorneys received $1,500,000 of this, leaving Michael with $3,000,000. I was very grateful to Bob Ludlow and his associate, Michael Moore, for making it possible for Michael to have this money. Without them, Michael would have received nothing.

While $3,000,000 seems like a great deal of money, I have found in the past five years that it is barely enough. $2,000,000 went into an annuity, which pays $9,800 a month and increases at a rate of 3% per year. Michael will receive this every month as long as he lives. $250,000 was invested in real estate, $500,000 in securities and $250,000 went for a special residential facility where Michael lived for 20 months. Due to the volatile stock market, even Michael's conservative investments lost money. Only the real estate investment has increased in value.

The $9,800 monthly payment is used entirely each month with the majority of it going to salaries for his attendants. I have hired a group of six people, most of whom work with Michael 13 hours a week. I also work 13 hours a week. I discovered that having people work longer with him was a sure path to burnout. Because it is hard on Michael when attendants change, my goal has been to find and RETAIN good people. In addition to the actual wages, expenses include payroll taxes, worker's compensation insurance, automobile insurance on Michael's van, unemployment insurance, wheelchair purchases and maintenance, physical therapy, food, rent, clothing, learning materials and outings. I also receive a small stipend as the trustee each month. Finally, because Michael has a court-ordered special needs trust, I must pay for the services annually of an accountant and attorneys. As part of the preparation for the law suit a professional social worker who specializes in needs assessments suggested that Michael would need at least $120,000 a year. She was right on!

I tell all of this because I want to impress on families that taking care of a severely disabled person can be very expensive. You will want to look carefully at the estimated costs before accepting any type of settlement or before signing away your right to sue.

In 1998 the Assisted Living Project received a gift of $250,000 from a single donor. Following a year of looking for the right property, the money was used to put a down payment on a house in Scotts Valley, California. The house is on Glenwood Drive and so is called Glenwood House. Michael, Michelle and three other residents moved in on December 15, 1999. In the years since 1996 Crystal and I have learned a great deal about how to set up a non-licensed residential home. In order to help others, we offer a workshop about replicating the model through the Central Coast Center for Independent Living,

Someone recently asked me what happened to Marty. Following our divorce in 1997 he went steadily downhill. In 2000 he was diagnosed with bladder cancer, which would have been highly treatable, if he had gone to the doctor sooner. He seemed to have given up on life and did little to fight the disease. He died in November 2000. He was not a psychologically strong man and I believe that Michael's accident and the numerous changes it brought to our lives were too much for him.

Michael remains happy for the most part. He shows slow, but steady, cognitive improvement. He is better today at holding a conversation and often asks if he can help with dishes or laundry. He sometimes surprises us with his memory. Recently he and I were in the grocery store where Cheerios were on sale. I wanted to get a box of regular Cheerios, but he wanted the sweetened ones. I prevailed. About 30 minutes later we were home and I asked Michael if he would like something to eat. He said, "yes, but not those regular Cheerios you bought!" I was absolutely amazed that he had re-membered!

Jody's Guide

The ideas presented here are gleaned from my ex-
perience with my son's accident, hospitals, medical pro-
fessionals, insurance companies and my family. I have
grouped the ideas by topic and have tried to make them
brief and easy to read. Many of them are discussed more
fully in the text. In parenthesis, I have indicated the
chapter where the discussion can be found.

1. *The really big ideas in this book*

- *A major traumatic injury to a loved one will sig-*
  nificantly change your family and your life.

- *Sooner, rather than later, contact an attorney.*

- *Sooner, rather than later, get a physiatrist on*
  your loved one's case. (3, 4)

- *The insurance company is formidable and con-*
  trolling. Make yourself known to them. Ask ques-
  tions. Ask for copies of correspondence, tell them

what you want and expect. Do not allow yourself to be "brushed off."

- *When your loved one moves from one hospital to another, make sure that the new facility has experience with the type of injury your loved one has.*

- *Work hard at being friendly and reasonable when interacting with the hospital staff. (4)*

2. *In the beginning (2, 3)*

- *Keep notes*

  As soon as possible get a notebook and some pens to leave at the hospital and try to identify a Family Information Officer who will write down important items and pass information to others in the family. During periods of high stress it can be difficult to focus on technical medical information, and therefore, writing key facts down can be very helpful. Information collected could include what doctors have said during their visits, notes on test results and up-coming tests, drugs being given and a list of medical terminology being used. The notebook can provide easy access to information when family members visit.

- *Visit the hospital library*

  Hospitals usually have libraries. A family member might visit and check out books related to the patient's condition or injury.

- *People react differently*

  Allow each person affected to find his/her own way through the crisis

  Remind yourself that each person is profoundly moved to do the very best that he or she can. Remind yourself that no one can carry another person through the tragedy.

- *Leave the bedside*

  Give yourself permission to go out of the room if medical procedures are happening to your loved one which are difficult for you.

- *Reduce surprises and stress*

  Call the hospital before you arrive to see what is going on and to prepare yourself.

  Stop at the nurses' station before going to the room to find out which nurse is working with your loved one and get an update in order to minimize surprises.

- *Collect yourself*

  Take a few minutes before you go into the room to collect yourself; meditate, take deep breaths, concentrate on bringing positive energy.

3. Working with the staff (3, 4)

- *To the fullest extent possible be considerate and grateful to the staff.*

- *Introduce yourself to everyone, including the housekeeping personnel.*

- *Keep a small notebook where you can write down peoples' names, descriptions and job functions.*

- *When you have a question or concern make every effort to speak to the staff person who covers that function so as not to waste the time of others.*

- *Greet staff by name and thank them for what they do for your loved one.*

- *Occasionally bring a treat to leave at the nurses station and, if possible, cover all three shifts.*

- *Periodically write a thank you note to the staff and leave it at the station.*

- *If you have access to flowers, bring some for the staff.*

- *Help where you can*
  If you are able, pitch in. Help change sheets, learn how to help position your loved one, learn where the dirty linen goes and take it there, learn where the clean linen is. Whenever possible, get things your loved one needs yourself. And certainly don't expect the staff to get you anything!

- *Remind yourself that there is no perfect hospital and no perfect staff.*

- *Request a change of physician*
  As a last resort, if you feel that your family isn't successful at communicating with your

loved one's doctor, you may request a change of physicians. When making the request, avoid specific criticisms and stick to the message that you have trouble communicating.

4. What you can do for your loved one during the acute hospital phase (2, 3, 4, 6)

- *Develop "A Visitors Guide" to help those who visit your loved one.*

Michael Bethune
A Visitor's Guide

Thank you

First, thank you so much for visiting Michael. It can be very difficult to visit a person who has suffered a severe injury. This guide has been developed to answer some questions and, hopefully, help you feel more comfortable being in the room with Michael.

The Accident

Michael and his best friend, Joe Lambinas, were in a car accident on August 20. They were traveling to the beach on highway 1 when they swerved to go around a car, hit the shoulder of the road, were forced across the highway and were hit by another car. Joe Lambinas was killed instantly.

The injuries

Michael, who is 22, has a severe brain injury. He was unconscious for 8 weeks and remains largely unresponsive. He is unable to speak or to move his body around. We do not know now and may not know for a long time if "he will get better."

In addition to the brain injury, Michael had severe lung injuries and a broken right hip. He has had frequent infections and he perspires profusely.

The equipment

One pole next to the bed has liquid food which is delivered directly to Michael's stomach. Michael has had a tracheotomy which is a surgical opening in his throat. The blue tube leading away from his neck provides oxygen and assists in breathing. Michael may be receiving medication through an IV line in one of his arms.

What to do when you visit

You can say hello to Michael and give him your name. You could talk about some times in the past when the two of you were together. You could talk about what you've been doing lately in your life. Since Michael likes both music and art, you might talk about one of these things. It is also fine to simply sit down and be present in the room. Before you go, please sign Michael's day-book which is on the table.

If you think something is wrong with Michael or the equipment, please call the nurse.

What's next for Michael?

We don't know at this time how long Michael will be at San Jose Medical Center. We are hopeful that he will progress enough to go to a sub acute hospital and then on to a rehabilitation facility.

Thank you again for visiting.

- Decorate your loved one's room.

- Consider taking a boom box and playing favorite music or taking favorite art or photographs.

- Develop and stick to a visitation schedule so that your loved one has maximum visitation time and also to get your family organized.

- Investigate and file for Short-term Disability, Medicare, Medicaid and Social Security benefits.

5. What you can do for yourself (3, 4, 6, 8)

- Check out the availability of a support group and, if there is one, visit.

- When you can't be at the hospital, call often and ask for a report on your loved one.

- *Make a list of the things you will need to feel comfortable at the hospital. Acquire those things and take them to your loved one's room.*

- *Consider taking a leave of absence from your job, if you are working. You may be eligible under the Family Leave Act.*

- *You may want to take some folding chairs to the hospital. Put your name on them.*

- *Acquire a file box and get your papers organized.*

6. *Identifying the best sub acute or rehabilitation hospital (4, 6, 8, 15)*

- *Ask the support group members for hospital recommendations.*

- *Visit*

  Visit the possible facilities on your list. Check to see if the floors are clean and the air smells good. Use the checklist below to ask questions. Also talk to a patient and ask what it is like to be there.

- *Questions to ask the In-take Manager of any facility you are considering for you loved one*

  What is the ratio of licensed nurses to patients? _____

  What is the ratio of CNAs to patients? _____

Are you currently fully staffed? _____

*Do you have a physician on staff? How
    often is he/she on the premises?* _____

*How long has this facility been in
    business? Who owns it?* _____

*How many patients do you currently
    have with an injury similar to my
    loved one?* _____

*How many patients have you had
    in the past year with a similar
    injury?* _____

*What has been the outcome for
    those patients?* _____

*What strategies have you developed for
    avoiding having patients discharged too
    soon?* _____

*What experience do you have in
    educating insurance companies and
    acquiring benefits to which patients
    may be entitled.* _____

*Why should we chose this facility over
    any other?* _____

7. *Effective strategies at the sub acute/ rehabilitation level (5, 6, 8, 9, 15)*

- *Create a guide*
    *Once a transfer has been made, create a
    guide for the new staff in working with your*

loved one so that you can share what you know and make the transition easier.

A Guide For The Staff Working With Michael Krizia

About Michael

Michael is a 23 year old man who resides in Scotts Valley in Santa Cruz County. The key word in describing Michael is "creative". From the time he was a small child, Michael has involved himself in creative pursuits. He is an accomplished multi-media artist. Although he is capable of producing very realistic work, he prefers abstract visual images in which he uses a variety of materials. He is very fond of color. Michael is also a creative musician who enjoys playing the piano and composing music. He likes listening to all kinds of music. His favorite singer is Joanie Mitchell. He is very fond of nature, especially the ocean, the Rocky Mountains and large rock formations. Michael is a respecter of all life. He is a very sensitive person who cares about animals and people in distress. Michael is also a private person who enjoys quiet time alone.

Professionally, Michael is a hair colorist and stylist. Here too he used his creativity, especially with color and became an expert in this field. He was employed at Jeanne Sumari Hair Design in Santa Cruz.

Michael's Family

Michael's older brother	David Bethune - lives in San Jose
David's partner	Joe Rodriguez - lives in San Jose
Michael's mother and dad	Jody and Marty Paterniti - live in Scotts Valley
Michael's maternal grandparents	Patty and Bill Cramer - live in Scotts Valley
Michael's biological father	David Bethune - lives in Arkansas
Woody, Otis and Alice	Family dogs
Kyle	Michael's cat

Since we have all these different last names we think of ourselves as a "nineties family". Michael's birth last name was Bethune, but when he was about 16 he decided that he wanted to change his last name. He selected Krizia and reported that there were no other "Krizias" in the telephone book. In time he got all his legal documents in this name and it became his legal last name.

There are three generations of our family closely involved with Michael's recovery and, therefore, expectations and attitudes represented by these different generations may become apparent to your staff. We will do our utmost to "get it together" and speak with one voice, however, we know from our experience at San Jose Medical Center and St. Luke's, that this is not always possible. If we are giving you conflicting messages, please let us know.

Michael's Accident

Michael was hurt in a car accident on Saturday, August 20. He and his best friend were going to the beach at Greyhound Rock near Davenport. Michael was driving the car north on highway 1. For some unknown reason he did not see a car that was stopped in his lane to make a left hand turn into a parking lot. In order to avoid hitting the stopped car, Michael went around the car on the right side, but the shoulder was very narrow and he lost control of his car, spinning out of control into traffic going south. He was hit from the back on the right side. Michael's friend was killed instantly. No one was hurt in the other vehicles. Michael was helicoptered by Calstar to San Jose Medical Center.

Michael sustained three major injuries:

- A severe closed head injury with multiple brain contusions
- A severe chest injury with multiple lung contusions
- A broken right hip

He was initially given a 5% chance to live. He was on a ventilator for 2 1/2 weeks, in a hard coma for 2 months and in San Jose Medical Center for 4 months. He spent 3 months at St. Luke's Subacute Hospital in San Leandro.

Michael has a shunt draining excess fluid from his brain to his abdominal cavity.

When Michael Asks About The Accident

If you happen to be with Michael when he asks about the accident, please tell him that he was in a car accident and he is now recovering in the hospital. It is unlikely that he will ask about his friend, Joe, but if he does, please tell him that Joe was killed and that he did not suffer. **If Michael doesn't say anything about Joe, we ask that the staff at Kentfield protect Michael from further agony by not mentioning Joe.**

What Works For Michael

Michael has periods of being agitated and restless. He may be uncomfortable with his position in bed or in the wheelchair and need a change. He may respond to some of his music tapes. He may respond to having someone speak calmly to him. He does not do well when there are a lot of people around him. He exhibits fear when he is transported from one area to another or transferred from bed to the wheelchair or back. Telling him ahead of time what is going to happen and talking to him during the transport can help. In general, we ask that you talk to Michael about what is happening as you would talk to any 23 year old man.

We ask you to be positive. We believe that Michael will get well. He has already come a great distance. We think of him as a hero… a winner… a champion. We ask you to bring positive attitudes with you when you work with him. We also ask that you bring laughter and a sense of humor.

In Conclusion

We have a great deal of confidence in Kentfield. We know that you will do all that you can for Michael. Thank you. We are here to help and support him and you in any way that we can. Tell us how we can help. If we are behaving in inappropriate or unhelpful ways, tell us. Please do not hesitate to be direct and honest with us. We look forward to our association with you.

- Identify a "designated brain" for the family.
- Find a "point person"
  Ask the hospital administrator to name a "point person" who will be your contact. This needs to be someone in the facility who can make decisions.

- Ask the hospital about "do's and don'ts" for families.

- *Get the rehabilitation guidelines*

  Get your hands on a copy of the rehabilitation guidelines the hospital uses so that you can ensure that your loved one receives maximum services and therapy time.

- *Be involved*

  Get involved with the treatment team. Attend therapy sessions and take notes. See if you can emulate some of the therapy techniques with your loved one on your own.

- *Addressing family concerns*

  Ask family members to write down their concerns and issues and to provide documented backup information such as day and time of event and the name of staff involved.

- *Sort problems by importance*

  With the help of the family "designated brain," sort issues and problems into two piles, "really important" and "let go of". For the really important issues, with documentation in hand, talk to the hospital "point person."

- *Take responsibility*

  Assume responsibility for being professional, polite and organized. Be on time for any and all meetings. Take notes so that information can be accurately shared with others in the family. If taking notes is difficult, ask if you can record the meeting on a small tape recorder.

- *Take supplies to the hospital so that you will be comfortable. Develop a way of leaving notes and information for other family members who visit.*

- *If you are having problems deciding whether or not to authorize a procedure or surgery, try to collect a variety of opinions, remembering that the goal of normalcy is very, very important.*

- *Work with the staff to come up with creative solutions to problems.*

- *If at all possible, take your loved one outside.*

- *Explore "complementary" or "alternative" medicine because western medicine does not have all the answers.*

- *Be assertive about discharge plans*

  Be assertive in working to prevent your loved one was being discharged too soon.

  Though they don't usually tell you, doctors have the ability to challenge the discharge decisions of insurance companies. Make sure the discharge decision is medically sound, not based on the insurance company's bottom line. You may need to have your attorney send a letter to the discharge planner stating that it wouldn't be wise to discharge your loved one at this time.

- *Remember: there is no perfect staff, no perfect hospital and no perfect family.*

8. When it's time for discharge (8, 15)

- Prior to discharge
  Ask the hospital case manager about all the optional things that happen to people when they leave the facility. Look into whether any of these are possible or desirable for your loved one.

- If your loved one won't be able to return home, try to find out where people with their disability live permanently. Visit these places and explore having your loved one go there.

- If there is no place for your loved one to live permanently, consider creating one.

- Let your elected officials know that you want options to nursing homes.

9. People with brain injuries (14)

Search for the right professional people to work with your loved one. Don't just assume the doctor, clinic or hospital will assign the right person.

It is your responsibility to create opportunities. You do not have the responsibility of making everything work out.

Talk to your loved one about the fact that their brain is like "Swiss cheese." Tell them that they can be a smart person with a disability or a crazy person, a bitter person, a defeated person, etc. Tell them that smart people with disabilities learn strategies for dealing with life and making adjustments.

10. Jody's hospital supply list (6)

Items I used in activities with Michael
A large plastic box with a lid for storing stuff
Several wooden puzzles
2" colored plastic blocks
"frog" bean bags or other small beanbags
Red, green, blue and yellow tempera paint
4 large paint brushes
White butcher paper
2 "paint shirts" - one for Michael, one for me
A plastic shower curtain (for protecting the floor)
A collection of visually interesting books (Michael especially responded to pop-up books)
Favorite video tapes
Paddles and a tennis ball covered with Velcro for playing "catch"
A collection of spices and herbs to smell
Miscellaneous supplies
Pens - permanent markers, ball point
Thumb tacks
½ wide transparent tape
2" wide transparent tape
Scissors
Note pads
An erasable message board for family use
Lysol or other room deodorant
Laundry detergent
Stain remover
Hangers
A camera and extra film

Folding chairs (hospitals all seem to have an absence
of chairs)
A flower vase
A jacket or sweater to leave at the hospital
Grooming supplies
A hairdresser's cape
Combs, hairbrush
Nail clippers
Moisturizing cream
Antibacterial liquid soap
A large hand mirror
Facial tissues
Vaseline
Baby powder
Large plastic container for catching shampoo water
Large plastic pitcher
Snack items
Reusable plastic drinking cups
Plastic forks and spoons
Cans or bottles of soft drinks
Cans of nuts
Crackers and cheese
One sharp knife
Cereal
Plastic bowls
Miniature candy bars
Other items
Because Michael was a musician he had a Yamaha
keyboard at Kentfield
Baskets for staff treats
Foil or plastic wrap for treats

11. *Activities I did with Michael (6)*

While he was in bed

- *We tossed around beanbags and foam rubber balls.*

- *We did "smelly things" in which Michael smelled one of a number of spices, herbs and flavorings. As his cognition improved, I added the dimension of having him smell something then offering a card with two options on it and asking him to point to the word that identified what he had smelled. I kept the collection of about 34 bottles and jars in a small plastic basket.*

- *I read Michael his favorite childhood stories. I also showed him pictures from visually interesting books such as pop-up books, without reading the text.*

- *We watched music videos and Michael's favorite Disney movies.*

When he was in the wheelchair

- *Using a hospital tray table, we worked puzzles. I bought a collection of wooden puzzles with "handles" on each piece for easy removal and replacement.*

- *I covered the tray table with butcher paper so that Michael could paint. At Toys R Us I discovered that there are these wonderful plastic "paint pots" that will virtually eliminate the problem of the paint container turning over spilling the contents. Michael used tempera paint and large brushes. I put a shower curtain down on the floor and placed* the wheelchair and the tray table over it. Michael wore an old shirt backward as a "paint shirt". I discovered that it was best if I wore one also!

- Again using the tray table, Michael worked with plastic blocks and Legos. It was helpful to cover the table with a towel because it made the surface less slippery.

- We did "tours" of the hospital noting the cafeteria, the family recreation room, the laundry room, the pharmacy room, the main lobby, and the physical and occupational therapy gyms.

12. Questions to ask an attorney you are considering engaging (15)

Do you handle personal injury cases? _____

How long have you been in this particular field? _____

Are you experienced in analysis of insurance health and liability policies? _____

Are you experienced in lien subrogation (reimbursement)? _____

Are you experienced in special needs trusts? _____

Do you have knowledge of public benefits? _____

Do you have experience with medical resources? _____

13. Things to consider if you want to create housing for your loved one (11)

- You will need four or five dedicated, committed people to work with you.

- You'll also need some seed money and the quickest way to get it is through donations.

- Think through the staff you'll need and write down specifically what each person is expected to do.

- In order to attract donors, you'll need IRS 501(c)3 status; until you are able to acquire it, some existing non-profit might take you under it's umbrella.

- Having a deadline can be a very good thing.

14. Job Description for Houseparent (11)

The house parents (houseparent) are employees of the Assisted Living Project and work in exchange for room and board. The county program, In Home Support Services, pays wages received. The House Manager supervises the house parents. While it is the goal of ALP to provide as much autonomy as possible for the house parents, they are subject to work direction from the House Manager or the Board of Directors.

Working largely independently, the house parents have oversight responsibility for the well being of the house residents, and the smooth operation of the house. The house parents are responsible for creating a "home" environment which includes, but is not limited to, facilitating interaction between residents, encouraging evenings of games and conversation, decorating the house, encouraging visits by family-members and friends of the residents. Houseparent should plan to interact regularly with both residents and the House Manager.

Houseparents are expected to maintain professional behavior in working with the various attendants at Glenwood. Each resident hires his or her own attendants so there may be variations in wages paid. Houseparents should not discuss wages with attendants. If Houseparents feel that a problem with an attendant exists, it is their responsibility to discuss this concern with either the House Manager or with the family of the resident, not with the various attendants.

Time off must be negotiated with the House Manager at least one week in advance. The house parents are entitled to 7 paid nights off (sick leave, vacation, personal business, bereavement) each year and may begin using the time after completing 4 months of employment. If nights off are taken during the first four months, the house parents will need to pay for a replacement person. In addition, if the house parents have used all 7 nights prior to completing a year of employment and take additional nights off, they will need to pay for a replacement person.

The ideal candidate is a couple with only one of them working outside the home. Ideal house parents are positive, proactive, compassionate and participatory in the house. In addition, they are proactive and posses "common sense" in problem solving situations.

Houseparent must be flexible as duties will change as the needs of residents change. The best interest of the residents is always priority, but house parents needs and concerns will, of course, be considered.

Glenwood is a drug free environment. Smoking must take place outside, preferably away from the house doors and windows. Houseparent may use alcohol responsibly, but not give any to residents.

Pets must be discussed with the House Manager prior to move in. Once living at Glenwood, the acquisition of new pets must be discussed with the House Manager. ALP expects that the cost of handling damage to the property by house parents' pets will be born by them.

Specific duties include, but are not limited to:

Being on the premises 5 days a week from 9 PM until 8 AM. Getting up at night to provide assistance to a resident(s) who needs it. This responsibility will vary depending on who lives at Glenwood and what their needs are, but house parents need to assume that someone will have to get up every four hours during the "duty" nights to assist one or more residents.

Being prepared to handle any nighttime emergency such as a fire or earthquake. Taking the appropriate action if a resident becomes ill *during the night. The house parents are there to provide a safe environment for the residents.*

Depositing residents' food checks into the household checking account and maintaining accurate records of expenses. Receipts are to be submitted to the House Manager by the 10th of the following month.

Preparing and posting a comprehensive menu on Sunday for each day of the upcoming week. When possible, preparing or offering a vegetarian option at dinner.

Purchasing food and supplies needed at the house, including food for dinners to be prepared by the attendants. Much research has gone into the best places to purchase house items and the house parents will be expected to do certain shopping at designated stores.

Preparing and participating in an evening meal 4/5 nights a week, joining residents at the dining table. The meal should be served at 5:30 PM and no later than 6:00 PM.

Interacting with residents at least two evenings (Mon – Fri) after dinner (conversation, watching a movie, playing a game.) This need not be all residents at one time.

Facilitating monthly house meetings (perhaps after dinner on a night when everyone is in attendance?) in which residents have an op-

portunity to discuss suggestions, chores and air complaints

Meeting on a regular basis with the House Manager and a member of the board of directors in order to discuss problems or issues.

Assigning household chores equally to all residents, keeping in mind their abilities. Attendants will assist those who are unable to complete their tasks or do the tasks on their behalf. It is the responsibility of the house parents to post the chore list and ensure that the chores are accomplished satisfactorily and in a timely fashion. In addition, house parents are responsible to instruct residents if they do not know how to accomplish a chore.

Working proactively with the House Manager to use money wisely by addressing such items as water leaks, improper use of the appliances, damage, wasteful habits on the part of the residents, etc.

Maintaining the lawn, which includes mowing, trimming, raking, watering, fertilizing.

Ensuring the watering of indoor plants, the vegetable and flowerbeds in order to assure that the plants flourish

Cleaning the carpets quarterly

Completing timecards and other paperwork in a timely fashion

Managing the collecting, bundling, sorting of garbage and assuring that the cans and recycled items are place at the curbside on the correct day

Cleaning the kitchen promptly after using it and maintaining a minimum of personal items in the shared spaces

Participating in ALP events such as Open Houses

We have read and understand the duties and responsibilities of being house parents at _____.

Signature   *Date*

_____

Signature   *Date*

15. *Job Description: Personal Attendant/ Companion for Michael Bethune (11)*

Reporting: *This position reports to Michael's mother, Jody Cramer*

It is expected that, except when specifically directed, you will give your full attention to Michael and the duties of this job during the entire duration of your shift.

Working without supervision, the Personal Attendant for Michael Bethune is expected to assume responsibility for all aspects of Michael's care, safety and well being while on the job. Job responsibilities include, but are not limited to:

- *Ensuring that Michael eats a healthy, well-balanced meal on each duty day, that he has a sufficient amount of liquids and that he eats so as not to gain weight*

- *Ensuring that Michael takes his medications completely and at the appropriate time*

- *Observing Michael in order to detect possible problems with the medications*

- *Interacting calmly and patiently with Michael. Working with him to encourage cognitive improvement through direct learning or the development of compensatory strategies. This includes playing games, using workbooks, reading aloud, discussing various subjects, writing together, making videos, exploring art and music, and structuring situations so that Michael can solve simple problems.*

- *Thinking "down the line" so as to anticipate what situations might cause Michael to be frustrated and working to manage the situations in such a way that Michael experiences minimal frustration. Planning ahead where his wheelchair will be able to easily go. The attendant is expected to use good judgment to solve problems whenever possible.*

- *Ensuring that Michael has on clean clothes*

- *Keeping accurate records on the daily report and academic reports.*

- *Appropriately using the weekly expense funds and staying within the budget, keeping receipts and preparing an expense report which is to be submitted at the end of each week*

- *Operating the vehicle Michael is in safely, following all rules of the road, including speed limits.*

- *Interacting positively with the other attendants, residents and the house parents at the Glenwood House.*

- *Helping Michael with social development so that he behaves appropriately in public*

- *Noting changes in Michael, which may signal that he is sick, alerting his mother*

- *Reporting any and all accidents to his mother, including falling from the bed or wheelchair, cuts or bruises, sunburns, etc.*

- *Taking responsibility for keeping the shared vehicle neat and clean, including removing used tissues, coffee cups, etc from your shift. Emptying, cleaning and replacing the van urinals, if they have been used on your shift*

- *The attendant is expected to try to find a substitute when he/she is sick by calling someone on the substitute list, preferably before the duty day.*

This position requires that the personal attendant posses patience, creativity, sensitivity, compassion, interpersonal skills and the ability to define goals and break them down into achievable steps. The personal attendant must also be punctual.

I have reviewed and understand this document:

_____

Signature   Date

16. Rancho Los Amigos Scale of Cognitive Functioning (2, 3)

1. No response:
    > Unresponsive to any stimulus.

2. Generalized response:
    > Limited, inconsistent, non-purpose-ful responses, often to pain only.

3. Localized response:
    > Purposeful responses; may follow simple commands; may focus on presented object.

4. Confused, agitated:
    > Heightened state of activity; confusion, disorientation; aggressive behavior; unable to do self-care; unaware of present events; agitation appears related to internal confusion.

5. Confused, inappropriate, non-agitated:
    > Appears alert; responds to commands; distractible; does not concen-

trate on task; agitated responses to external stimuli; verbally appropriate; does not learn new information.

6. *Confused, appropriate:*

Good directed behavior, needs cueing; can relearn old skills as Activities of Daily Living (ADL); serious memory problems; some awareness of self and others.

7. *Automatic appropriate:*

Robot-like appropriate behavior, minimal confusion, shallow recall; poor insight into condition; initiates tasks but needs structure; poor judgment, problem-solving and planning skills.

8. *Purposeful appropriate:*

Alert, oriented; recalls and integrates past events; learns new activities and can continue without supervision; independent in home and living skills; capable of driving; defects in stress tolerance, judgment, abstract reasoning persist; many function at reduced levels in society.

About the Author

Jody Cramer has a unique insight into how families are affected by serious trauma. She lived it. *An Excellent Life* is her first book and was written out a desire to help other families. Jody lives in California and devotes most of her time to caring for her severely disabled son and managing the non-profit she co-founded.

Her website is JodyCramer.com

Printed in the United States
79626LV00001B/39